For more information,
please visit *gestalten.com*

Bibliographic information
published by the Deutsche
Nationalbibliothek: The Deutsche
Nationalbibliothek lists this
publication in the Deutsche
Nationalbibliografie; detailed
bibliographic data are available
online at *dnb.d-nb.de*

	MIX
	Paper from responsible sources
FSC www.fsc.org	FSC® C011712

This book was printed on
paper certified by the FSC®

Monocle editor in chief
and chairman: *Tyler Brûlé*
Monocle editor: *Andrew Tuck*
Books editor: *Joe Pickard*
Guide editor: *Chloë Ashby*

Designed by *Monocle*
Proofreading by *Monocle*
Typeset in *Plantin & Helvetica*

Printed by *Offsetdruckerei
Grammlich, Pliezhausen*

Made in Germany

Published by *Gestalten*, Berlin 2019
ISBN 978-3-89955-971-2

© Die Gestalten Verlag GmbH &
Co. KG, Berlin 2019

The MONOCLE
Travel Guide Series

Chicago

Welcome
—— Making it
in the Midwest

"Chicago is the great American city," says Norman Mailer in his 1968 report on that year's state of US politics, *Miami and the Siege of Chicago*. It may have originally struggled to compete with the big hitters on the east and west coasts but today it's carved out an identity of its own that brings together the best of both – including a handful of *sandy beaches*.

This *Midwest marvel* is the birthplace of the skyscraper and home to *bold and brilliant architecture* by world-renowned figures from Mies van der Rohe to Frank Lloyd Wright. Closer to ground, it's peppered with first-rate museums and *public art* by the likes of Calder and Chagall – as well as urban art by talented residents. And that's not to mention the giggle-a-minute *comedy clubs* and bluesy *jazz bars*.

Chicago is at once international and local, lofty and down to earth, with a laid-back boutique for every luxury fashion house and a classic US diner (complete with spinning stools and bright bulbs) for every immaculately designed, Asian-inspired restaurant. It supports *small businesses* and treasures the old as well as the new, with family-run hotels cropping up in *classic heritage buildings*.

Located on the southwest shore of Lake Michigan, Chicago has a *coastal feel* while still being very much a Midwest metropolis. It's far from perfectly polished – with that *grumbling L train* and one too many places serving *deep-dish pizza* – and that's partly why we like it. It's American in the best possible way. As Mailer continues, "Perhaps it is the last of the great American cities." — (M)

Contents
—— Navigating the city

Use the key below to help navigate the guide section by section.

 H Hotels

 F Food and drink

 R Retail

 T Things we'd buy

 E Essays

C Culture

D Design and architecture

S Sport and fitness

 W Walks

Map
— Lay of
the land

It may be in the Midwest
but Chicago, in northern
Illinois, feels far from
landlocked. Cosying up
to the southwest shore
of Lake Michigan, and
with the Chicago River
running through it, the
Windy City feels at once
cosmopolitan and coastal.

After it was first
recognised as a city at
the swampy mouth of
the Chicago River in
1837, it expanded at a
startling rate in the 19th
century – partly thanks to
significant infrastructure
improvements. Today it
sprawls both along the
lake and inland to the
west, with a population
of almost three million
and a reputation for
being one of the biggest
transportation hubs in
the US (with one of the
busiest airports in the
world to boot).

Join us as we traverse
the city, from the industrial
warehouses of the
south and the bohemian
boutiques in the west
to the tree-lined avenues
of the residential north
and the cluster of
gleaming skyscrapers in
the east. We hope you
packed some comfy
footwear – it's time to
pound those pavements.

EDGEWATER

ANDERSONVILLE

LINCOLN
SQUARE

UPTOWN

ALBANY
PARK

IRVING
PARK

NORTH
CENTER

Wrigley Field

AVONDALE

LAKEVIEW

LINCOLN PARK

LOGAN
SQUARE

BUCKTOWN

WICKER
PARK

HUMBOLDT
PARK

GOOSE
ISLAND

OLD
TOWN

GOLD
COAST

UKRAINIAN
VILLAGE

NOBLE
SQUARE

EAST
VILLAGE

RIVER
WEST

WEST TOWN

Frank Lloyd Wright
Home and Studio

WEST LOOP

GARFIELD
PARK

NEAR
WEST SIDE

UNIVERSITY
VILLAGE /
LITTLE ITALY

SOUTH LOOP

PILSEN

EAST
PILSEN

LOWER WEST SIDE

ARMOUR
SQUARE

BRIDGEPORT

Stony Island Arts Bank

McCormick Tribu
Campus Cente

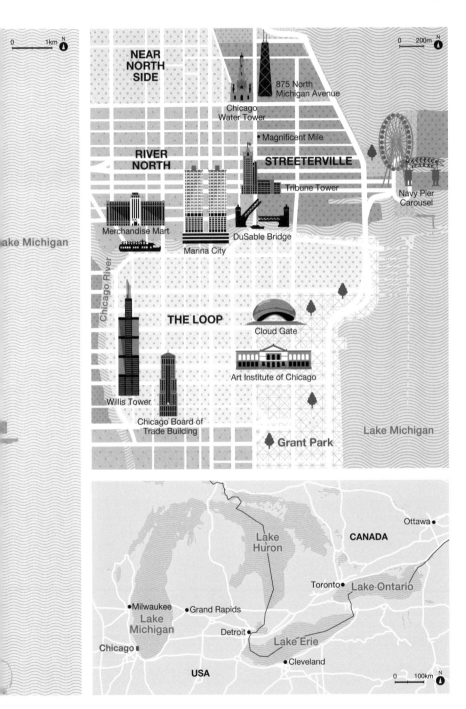
Chicago
Map

NEAR
NORTH
SIDE

875 North
Michigan Avenue

Chicago
Water Tower

RIVER
NORTH

Magnificent Mile

STREETERVILLE

Tribune Tower

ake Michigan

Merchandise Mart

DuSable Bridge

Marina City

Navy Pier
Carousel

Chicago River

THE LOOP

Cloud Gate

Art Institute of Chicago

Willis Tower

Chicago Board of
Trade Building

Grant Park

Lake Michigan

Lake
Huron

CANADA

Ottawa

Toronto   Lake Ontario

Milwaukee   Grand Rapids

Lake
Michigan

Detroit

Lake Erie

Chicago

Cleveland

USA

0   100km

Need to know
—— Get to grips with the basics

History
Rollercoaster ride

Since first being recognised as a city in 1837, Chicago has had its ups and downs. Migrants from the East Coast set the footing for prosperity and a strong workforce over the following decades but the Great Chicago Fire of 1871, which razed much of the city, nipped this growth in the bud. From the rubble rose a new cityscape and in the 1880s the world's first skyscraper sprung up here (*see page 111*). In 1893 the Chicago World's Fair put the city in the global spotlight and accelerated its progressive thinking.

The early 20th century brought further economic growth but also the rise of the criminal underworld, with gangsters such as Al Capone capitalising on the Prohibition era of 1919 to 1933. The Great Depression took hold between 1929 and 1939 but still the city stood strong and migration during the Second World War diversified society. This sparked debates surrounding race, and often conflict, but from the chaos has risen social progress – enter Barack Obama, a former senator of Illinois. Today Chicago walks firmly in the vanguard of US culture, business and politics.

Baseball
Pick a team

There are two Major League Baseball teams in Chicago: the Cubs (who won the World Series in 2016) and the White Sox (who won in 2005). Chicagoans have incredibly strong feelings about the team they support and you won't find anyone who cheers for both. Geographically, Cubs fans tend to live on the northern side of the city while Sox fans are located on the south and west sides. The key is to choose your team and then stick with it.

Transport
Track record

Chicago's public transport revolves around the L train, which has eight lines and goes to just about every neighbourhood in the city. It's inexpensive, easy to navigate and relatively fast (if there aren't any issues).

While most of the trains run late into the evening, and some even operate 24 hours a day, it's best to avoid hopping aboard after 21.00. Switch to a taxi after dark for safety.

Um, aren't we supposed to be on that train?

Nicknames
Terms of endearment

Chicago has its fair share of nicknames, which could do with some elucidation. The "Windy City" may seem self-explanatory – just step outside and feel that off-the-back-of-the-lake breeze – but some say it stems from the city's supposedly boastful nature and long-winded political speeches in the late 19th century. The "Second City" has shed its negative connotations (it was coined as an insult by New Yorker AJ Liebling in 1952) and today is more kindly taken to mean "second to none". Finally, the "City of Big Shoulders" comes from Carl Sandburg's poem "Chicago" while "That Toddling Town" is lifted from Frank Sinatra's song of the same name.

Weather
Seasons change

If you're planning a trip to Chicago, be prepared for anything: the temperature can plummet from 20C to 0C in a single day. If you want to make the most of the city beaches, come in summer – but bear in mind it can be hot and sticky. At the other end of the spectrum, in winter you may be greeted with heavy snowfall. Spring is often the wettest time of year so don't forget your umbrella.

We recommend autumn: the summer crowds have subsided, the cold has yet to take hold and the golden leaves are still clinging onto the trees. At the end of October you'll be in for a show: Chicagoans – like many residents in the US – take Halloween very seriously.

Neighbourhoods
In the zones

Google "Chicago landmarks" and your search will throw up an array of skyscrapers mainly in and north of the Loop – the hub of big business and luxury shopping. Head north and you'll find Lincoln Park, a residential zone named after the city's largest patch of green, while further north still are similarly lived-in Lakeview and the design-savvy Andersonville.

To the west is Wicker Park, beloved by art and music fans, and beyond it Logan Square, a hub for wining and dining. Then there are the districts down south, from the warehouse-heavy South Loop to Pilsen, with its plethora of Mexican murals.

Despite its reputation Chicago is generally safe but there are, of course, certain neighbourhoods to avoid. We suggest you steer clear of Fuller Park and the surrounding area and, as always, take extra care at night wherever you are.

Lake Michigan
Shore winner

The fresh-water Lake Michigan is the fifth-largest lake in the world. In summer, residents flock to the 26 city beaches dotted along its shore, each of which has its own particular pull – from bars to volleyball (*see page 128*). The waterfront trails crawl with joggers and cyclists while paddle-boarders and swimmers take to the lake (*see page 129*).

Opening hours
About time

For a city of its size, it's surprising that long opening hours aren't necessarily a given. A number of restaurants, museums and live venues are closed on Mondays, while some retailers (especially those located outside the city centre) shut up shop on Tuesdays.

Brunch is big in Chicago so be prepared to wait in line if you come at peak time (between 09.00 and 11.00 on a Sunday). Most bars are open until about 02.00. If you plan on dropping by a commercial gallery, it's best to check the hours online.

Etiquette
Skip the ketchup

Chicago-style hot dogs, topped with yellow mustard, fried onions, relish, a couple of tomato slices, a pickle and a sprinkling of celery salt, are famous the world over. But don't even think about asking for ketchup when you order: there's a decent chance you'll be kicked out of a restaurant for that faux pas. In Chicago, ketchup has no place on a hot dog. Why? Because it's perfect as it is, of course.

Another rule when it comes to Chicago restaurants – and taxis, hairdressers, spas and salons, for that matter – is to tip about 20 per cent. (If in doubt, double the tax.) Just in case you're not used to the US method, the waiter will take your card and return it with a receipt, on which you write the tip and sign after paying.

Our top picks:

01 Publishing House B&B: Eleven design-savvy rooms in the industrial West Loop. *see page 14*

02 Lula Café: Leading player in Logan Square's dining scene. *see page 33*

03 Frank Lloyd Wright Home and Studio: Explore the home and work space of the world-renowned US architect. *see page 119*

04 Blind Barber: Four-chair barbershop with a speakeasy to boot. *see page 127*

05 The iO Theater: Laugh-until-you-cry improv. *see page 98*

06 Heritage Bicycles General Store: Freshly brewed coffee and vintage-inspired bikes. *see page 50*

07 The Peninsula Spa: Take five (or more) in this luxury spa. *see page 125*

08 Art Institute of Chicago: Home to Grant Wood's "American Gothic" and more. *see page 92*

09 Martha Mae: Light-filled art supplies and everyday tools shop. *see page 51*

10 Scofflaw: Gin-focused cocktail bar. Need we say more? *see page 49*

This hot dog is well stuffed. And so is my lunch

Hotels
—— Get a room

Chicago welcomes some 55 million people a year, and is the city break of choice for US residents, so it should come as no surprise that it has its fair share of good hotels. After an extended pause in construction following the financial crisis in 2008 the city has been churning out places to stay at an unprecedented rate – and an array of hospitality groups have been repurposing classic Chicago buildings.

The UK-based Soho House & Co opened an outpost in a former warehouse in 2014 and The Robey set up shop in an art deco office block two years later. There are also rooms in a former publishing house, a historic athletic association and a modernist skyscraper by Mies van der Rohe for good measure.

Chicago has a whole host of hotels that will do the job. If you want to stay in the lap of luxury, join the glitterati at the star-studded stop-ins in the Loop. Meanwhile, if you're after something with a more independent feel, check out some of our family-run options.

1

Publishing House B&B,
West Loop
Fully booked

Every detail in this beautiful city bolthole has been carefully considered, from the fresh pastries in the butler's pantry to the Malin+Goetz products in each en-suite bathroom. Co-owners Shawn Uldridge and Kimberly Lowery – keep an eye out for their pugs, Angus and Louie – sourced the modern and vintage furniture themselves. "We spent two years travelling around the US to flea markets, antiques shops and auctions," says Lowery.

The pair moved from Melbourne to Chicago in 2014 and opened the 11-room Publishing House three years later. The name stems from the building's original purpose: it started life in 1909 as the Free Methodist Publishing House.
108 North May Street, 60607
+1 312 554 5857
publishinghousebnb.com

MONOCLE COMMENT: Each bedroom is named after a Chicago-based author or an element in their book. Rooney is quiet and cosy while Carmen features framed nudes drawn by Uldridge and Lowery.

②
The Robey, Wicker Park
Top drawer

Belonging to the impressive portfolio of Mexico-based Grupo Habita, The Robey is a celebration of Chicago's fine architectural history, housed in a soaring wedge of a tower block from 1929 and the adjoining brick warehouse. The 89-room hotel has been through a few reconfigurations since it first moved to Wicker Park in 2016 but it became an instant neighbourhood anchor: crowds of locals and visitors alike sip cocktails at the rooftop bar or tuck into brunch in the American bistro-style restaurant on the ground floor.

The interiors – which marry original art deco features with mid-century accents, giving the property the air of a moody Edward Hopper painting – come courtesy of Belgian design duo Nicolas Schuybroek Architects and Marc Merckx Interiors. Oh, and there's a small pool open to the public.
2018 West North Avenue, 60647
+1 872 315 3050
therobey.com

MONOCLE COMMENT:
According to urban legend, a Prohibition-era tunnel leads from The Robey to the basement of a neighbouring bar: proof that the property has long known how to let its hair down.

❸
Soho House, West Loop
Buckle up

The UK-based hospitality firm Soho House & Co moved into this former belt factory in 2014. In doing so, it helped transform the former meatpacking district into one of the city's hottest postcodes.

Hotel guests and Soho House members have access to a 1920s-inspired gym, a screening room and a rooftop space with a swimming pool. There are also myriad spaces open to the public: the ground-floor Allis (*see page 40*) is a popular brunch spot and we like the cosiness of the Fox Bar, the late-night boozer upstairs. All 40 bedrooms feature king-sized beds and custom-designed wallpaper.
113-125 North Green Street, 60607
+1 312 521 8000
sohohousechicago.com

MONOCLE COMMENT:
There are more than 250 pieces of original art on display throughout the property.

④
Ace Hotel, West Loop
Joint effort

As with all Ace Hotels, the Chicago outpost works with the surrounding community. Alongside the exhibitions by local artists in the ground-floor gallery, works by students hang in the 159 bedrooms. Other "Made in Chicago" details include flowers by Bottle & Branch and home accessories made with Horween Leather.

The Ace opened in mid-2017 and was renovated by Los Angeles-based Commune Design. Inspired by Chicago's New Bauhaus school of design, the concrete-and-glass building is accented with polished steel and perforated brass. Hand-woven textiles such as the geometric blankets on the beds – king-size in all but the double rooms – add a touch of warmth.
311 North Morgan Street, 60607
+1 312 764 1919
acehotel.com/chicago

MONOCLE COMMENT: If you're on a whirlwind visit, the Ace has you covered. City Mouse offers seasonal Midwest-inspired fare, Waydown serves sharp cocktails and Stumptown Coffee Roasters has some of the best beans in town.

Ⓢ
The Freehand, River North
High-end hostel

A hostel may not be your
natural first choice but that's
because you haven't stayed at
The Freehand yet. This hotel-
hostel hybrid offers private and
shared rooms that sleep up to
four people – but don't expect
the usual rickety bunk beds and
bathroom-down-the-corridor
backpacker experience.

The 1920s building in which
The Freehand is housed has
been beautifully redesigned
by Roman and Williams,
inspired by Lake Michigan,
and has a laid-back vintage
Midwest feel. You'll find
cocktails, live music and
DJs at the Broken Shaker
downstairs, while Café Integral
is on hand for your morning
caffeine fix or a quick bite.
This hotel isn't afraid of a good
time and is the perfect place
for people who want to explore
Chicago's late-night scene and
enjoy a nightcap before bed.
*19 East Ohio Street, 60611
+1 312 940 3699
freehandhotels.com/chicago*

MONOCLE COMMENT:
Stay in the penthouse suite,
where visiting rockstars have
been known to throw parties.

(6)
Thompson Chicago,
Gold Coast
Reliable rooms

Located in the ritzy Gold
Coast, this property by the
dependable Thompson chain
opened in 2013 and is a solid
choice for business travellers
or those wanting easy access to
the area's upmarket boutiques.
The hotel's 247 rooms make
the most of city views with
floor-to-ceiling windows, many
offering glimpses of Lake
Michigan – Oak Street Beach
is at the end of the block. The
ground-floor Italian restaurant
Nico Osteria is a popular spot
for breakfast, lunch and dinner.
21 East Bellevue Place, 60611
+1 312 266 2100
thompsonhotels.com

MONOCLE COMMENT:
The so-called Secret Stairway
is splashed with the work of
some of Chicago's best street
and graffiti artists – a contrast
to the sleek look employed by
interior designer Tara Bernerd
throughout the rest of the hotel.

The Four Seasons, Gold Coast
Top to bottom

Located near the Magnificent Mile (prime location for luxury retailers and restaurants) in one of Chicago's tallest towers, The Four Seasons offers panoramic views of the city and Lake Michigan. This classic hotel comprises 160 rooms and 185 suites; we would recommend the executive suite for a particularly spacious stay (ask for the highest one possible). The hotel also boasts a spa and nail salon where you can kick back and indulge in a treatment or two.
*120 East Delaware Place, 60611
+1 312 280 8800
fourseasons.com/chicago*

MONOCLE COMMENT: The view from the top may be a highlight but head down to the lower levels to use the pool, which featured in *Home Alone 2*.

⑦
Longman & Eagle, Logan Square
Inn style

A year after opening their bar and restaurant (*see page 39*) in 2010, the quartet behind Longman & Eagle transformed it into an inn by adding six bedrooms above. Each is simply furnished and retains its exposed-brick walls and unpolished floorboards. But that's not to say they've skimped on the finer details.

Room 55 is our favourite, with a king-sized bed, a freestanding bathtub and a white-tiled walk-in shower stocked with Aesop. Whichever room you choose, just bear in mind you're sleeping above a popular – and potentially noisy – neighbourhood haunt.
*2657 North Kedzie Avenue, 60647
+1 773 276 7110
longmanandeagle.com*

MONOCLE COMMENT: You can order room service from the restaurant and, when you arrive, you'll be given two drink tokens to redeem at the bar.

9

Kimpton Gray Hotel,
The Loop
All the gear

A Chicago landmark, The New York Life Insurance Building was transformed into a hotel by the Kimpton group in 2016. It sits at 15 storeys high right in the heart of the Loop.

The hotel has a spa and a fitness centre complete with state-of-the-art equipment; guests can borrow Lululemon gym clothes from the front desk (handy if you've packed lightly for a quick business trip). Bikes are free for all to use but make sure you get back in time for wine hour at 17.00, when you can enjoy a complimentary glass of chardonnay in the lobby. Later, grab a bite to eat at Boleo, the Latin American rooftop bar and restaurant.
122 West Monroe Street, 60603
+1 312 750 9012
grayhotelchicago.com

MONOCLE COMMENT:
This is a pet-friendly hotel for those who like to travel with their pooch.

(10)
Chicago Athletic Association Hotel, The Loop
Be a sport

This Venetian gothic marvel overlooking Millennium Park was built in 1893 as a members-only men's club for the Chicago Athletic Association, which it remained until 2007. The hotel in its place is an ode to the building's history, featuring lifts lined with original fencing floors, wooden carvings depicting sportsmen who graced the club throughout the years, and a basketball court.

Paintings and trophies discovered in the building have been reinstalled as part of the hotel's decor. If you look closely you'll find a familiar logo dotted around: the "C" of the Chicago Athletic Association was supposedly modified for the Chicago Cubs.
12 South Michigan Avenue, 60603
+1 844 312 2221
chicagoathletichotel.com

MONOCLE COMMENT:
Don't leave without grabbing a drink in the Milk Room, a Prohibition-era speakeasy turned eight-seat bar serving vintage and rare spirits.

Luxury lodgings

01 The Ritz-Carlton Chicago, Streeterville: Housed in the historic Water Tower Place on the Magnificent Mile, The Ritz-Carlton reopened in 2017 after multi-million dollar renovation works. Slip into the snuggest of hotel robes and admire the sweeping views of the city and lake from the comfort of your bedroom. *ritzcarlton.com*

02 The Peninsula Chicago, River North: The journey isn't over when you reach this international powerhouse: book a suite and you can zip around the city in one of the hotel's bespoke Mini Cooper S Clubman cars. Other perks: the rooftop Z Bar, the indoor pool and spa (*see page 125*), and that decadent afternoon tea in the lobby. *peninsula.com*

03 The Langham Chicago, River North: This landmark structure by Mies van der Rohe is a modern marvel of steel and glass. Since 2013 it has housed the Chicago outpost of The Langham, with 268 bedrooms and 48 suites. *langhamhotels.com*

I'll be honest, this beats sleeping on a branch

Food and drink
—— Taste of Chicago

To outsiders, Chicago's food scene is known for a few things: gargantuan deep-dish pizzas, hot dogs decked out with tomatoes and pickles (anything but ketchup) and, on the flip side, a highly regarded fine-dining culture. To Chicagoans, the city's food scene is all that and so much more.

It's a city that offers delicious dining at every price point, where cheeseburgers are as highly sought after as brown butter-basted rib-eye steaks. The city has a large Mexican population and, as such, tacos are an art form. Chefs from elsewhere have contributed global dishes such as Roman pizza, Louisiana fried chicken and Vietnamese coffee and banh mi.

Much of Chicago's dining scene is centred around the two hubs of the West Loop and Logan Square, where you'll find a mix of restaurants along with excellent coffee shops and cocktail bars – so they're great places to start your culinary explorations. But to truly eat like a Chicagoan, all you need to do is arrive with an open mind and an empty stomach – then dig in.

1

Table, Donkey and Stick, Logan Square
Alpine state

The sparing tagline for this restaurant is "Crusty Bread, Brandy, Fire" and it sums up the place perfectly. "The seasonal menu is built around old-world traditions of bread-baking, charcuterie and preservation, applied to products of the Midwest," says proprietor and sommelier Matt Sussman, who has assembled an excellent wine list drawn from the Alpine regions. On the menu are dishes such as potato latkes with horseradish aioli, duck-liver mousse, and a burger with fontina and cranberry *mostarda* (an Italian condiment) tucked into a pretzel bun.
2728 West Armitage Avenue, 60647
+1 773 486 8525
tabledonkeystick.com

②
Pacific Standard Time,
River North
California dreaming

California is chef Erling
Wu-Bower's major source of
inspiration and he transports
it to Pacific Standard Time
by emulating the state's free-
spirited vibe and vegetable-
focused food. The design of
the light-filled space – with
terrazzo and wooden floors,
lots of foliage, and white walls
– completes the West Coast
feel. This place is equally suited
to a lively dinner with friends
as a business lunch with clients.

Two wood-burning ovens
turn out fluffy pitta served with
hummus or marinated ahi tuna,
as well as blistered pizzas such
as a margherita accented with
preserved *giardiniera* (a zingy
Italian relish). Fresh salads
and perfectly cooked seafood
and meat dishes round off the
menu, enhanced by a wine list
that leans toward the Golden
State and Old World tipples.
141 West Erie Street, 60654
+1 312 736 1778
pstchicago.com

3

Elske, West Loop
Scandi crush

Elske means "love" in Danish and Denmark is at the root of chefs Anna (*pictured*) and David Posey's West Loop restaurant. Complete with exposed brick walls and mid-century modern furniture, it's a lovely minimalist spot for lingering over a meal that draws from both Scandinavian and Midwest traditions.

Whether you choose the tasting menu or order à la carte, the dishes are seasonal and beautifully presented – from the slice of duck-liver tart served with salted ramps (wild garlic) to the soft-scrambled eggs with mushrooms and kale, and the sunflower-seed parfait drizzled with sour honey. Toast your meal with a glass of homemade schnapps, which comes in flavours such as dill or black raspberry.
1350 West Randolph Street, 60607
+1 312 733 1314
elskerestaurant.com

④
Proxi, West Loop
World tour

Chef Andrew Zimmerman made his name at the excellent West Loop restaurant Sepia; next door is Proxi, his second restaurant and a visual stunner with flavours to match. "Proxi's menu was inspired by both my travels abroad and my time right here in Chicago," he says. "I've always been drawn to bold, vibrant flavours, and regularly find new dish ideas while exploring Chicago's rich culinary scene."

The menu includes Asian, Middle Eastern and Mexican influences in dishes such as tempura *elotes* (grilled corn) and black-pepper pork, and Sarah Mispagel's tempting desserts are equally inventive. The design is sleek, with floor-to-ceiling windows, antique mirrors, leather booths and vibrant tiles. One for a must-impress meeting or sealing that business deal.
565 West Randolph Street, 60661
+1 312 466 1950
proxichicago.com

⑤
BoeufHaus, Humboldt Park
Steak a claim

Chicago is a steak town and no one does the job quite like chef Brian Ahern (*pictured*). His intimate BoeufHaus takes cues from traditional French and German recipes for dishes such as short-rib beignets or the beef tartare stirred up with capers, shallots and Dijon, and served with brioche.

The 55-day, dry-aged ribeye comes with Bordelaise, béarnaise or au poivre sauces; pescatarians, meanwhile, have options such as celery-cured Arctic char and Alaskan halibut with chanterelles, mussels and ginger. Be sure to grab a seat at the cosy copper-topped bar for a pre-dinner martini or German draft beer.
1012 North Western Avenue, 60622
+1 773 661 2116
boeufhaus.com

Fat Rice, Logan Square
Ticket to Macau

If you haven't tried Macanese cuisine – which fuses Chinese, Portuguese, African and other influences – Fat Rice is a great place to start. Chef Abe Conlon serves dishes such as chilli prawns with garlic and fermented black beans, pork-and-ginger dumplings with sweet soy and chilli oil, and *arroz gordo* (the eponymous fat rice, which comes packed with curried chicken, barbecued pork, linguiça and more).

Fat Rice also has an adjacent bakery – try the snickerdoodle (a cookie) with salted-yolk custard filling – and a bar, Ladies' Room, where globally inspired cocktails are created with homemade ingredients.
2957 West Diversey Avenue, 60647
+1 773 661 9170
eatfatrice.com

Parachute, Avondale
Korea highlight

At Parachute, Beverly Kim and Johnny Clark put a satisfying spin on traditional Korean food, with plates such as bibimbap with yellowfin tuna or kale-and-beef stew with sweet potatoes. The seasonal menu changes regularly but the baked-potato *bing* bread – stuffed with spring onions, cheddar and bacon, and served with sour-cream butter – is a firm fixture.

A communal table runs down the middle of the long and slender space, which is lined on one side with exposed bricks. The drinks list is stellar, with wines, ciders, sakés and more helping to make a night at Parachute a convivial one.
3500 North Elston Avenue, 60618
+1 773 654 1460
parachuterestaurant.com

⑧
Daisies, Logan Square
Fresh from the farm

The succinct menu at Daisies comprises handmade pastas (think beetroot agnolotti with dill), daily-changing starters and crowd-pleasers such as crispy fried mushrooms and cheese curds with buttermilk-tarragon dipping sauce.

Owner and executive chef Joe Frillman (*pictured, on left*) sources much of the produce for his vegetable-focused dishes from his family farm, and adheres to what he calls the "Italian philosophy" of using what's in season in a simple way. "Our daily inspiration is derived from the question: If the Midwest were a region in Italy, what would the food look like?" he says.
2523 North Milwaukee Avenue, 60647
+1 773 661 1671
daisieschicago.com

Pizza perfection

01 Pizzeria Bebu, Goose Island: The crust at Pizzeria Bebu is a work of art; crispy on the bottom with a chewy edge, it's the perfect vessel for toppings that range from classic (a pitch-perfect margherita) to creative (an everything-bagel crust pie with caramelised onion, house-cured pancetta and an egg). Can't decide? Try a half-and-half option with two different toppings. *bebu.pizza*

02 Spacca Napoli Pizzeria, Uptown: With an oven straight from Naples, the pizzas at Spacca Napoli are a worthy ode to the Neapolitan style: thin pies with soft centres and restrained toppings that are all about quality. The cheeseless marinara puts tomatoes front and centre while the puttanesca gets some salty funk from anchovies, black olives and capers. *spaccanapolipizzeria.com*

03 Bonci Pizzeria, West Loop: Roman *pizzaiolo* Gabriele Bonci opened his first US outpost in Chicago in 2017 and serves his Roman-style pizzas *al taglio* (by weight). Choose from the 20 pizza options regularly on offer – with toppings such as nduja and burrata or spicy aubergine – and a pizza-maker will snip a slice for you with scissors. You can select the size so it's easy to try a number of different-flavoured slices in one sitting. *bonciusa.com*

9

Band of Bohemia,
Lincoln Square
Brewing up a storm

The decor in this softly lit
former Oreo factory may be a
tad eccentric (velvet chairs and
elephant-print curtains) but
the brewery-cum-coffee-shop-
cum-restaurant is popular with
visitors and residents alike.

Band of Bohemia offers
a smart five-course tasting
menu along with mainstays
such as carrot lasagne or
kurobuta pork with smoked
heirloom grits, Brussels sprouts
kraut, fermented rye and
uni (sea urchin) butter. The
drinks list caters to all tastes
and features in-house beers,
excellent cocktails (alcoholic
and non) and a top-notch
wine list.
*4710 North Ravenswood Avenue,
60640*
+1 773 271 4710
bandofbohemia.com

Must-try
Chorizo-stuffed medjool
dates from Avec, West Loop
The stuffed dates on Avec's
Mediterranean-focused
menu are a cult favourite for
a reason. Stuffed with spicy
fresh chorizo, wrapped in
crispy bacon and served
on a piquillo pepper-tomato
sauce, the dates are salty,
sweet, tangy and meaty.
avecrestaurant.com

⑩
Pequod's Pizza, Lincoln Park
Dive into deep dish

This Lincoln Park staple has been serving its thick-pan pizzas for more than 25 years. The secret to the continued success (and the long wait for a table) is in the caramelised crust: a thin layer of cheese along the exterior gives the pie a chewy edge and extra flavour.

For toppings, sausage and pepperoni are classic Chicago. Or you can cut down on the wait by sneaking in for the $4.95 weekday cheese-pizza lunch special.

2207 North Clybourn Avenue, 60614
+1 773 327 1512
pequodspizza.com

Blackbird, West Loop
Top flight

Executive chef Paul Kahan's Midwestern food is bursting with fresh produce and brilliant flavour combinations. Dishes are offered à la carte or as part of a 10-course tasting menu and include roasted lamb saddle with red grapefruit and Brussels sprouts; grilled sturgeon with ramp kimchi and mustard greens; and barbecued pork belly with black garlic, mushrooms and smoked trout roe.

The pared-back design – with muted tones, white tablecloths and monochrome artwork by Chicago-based Lonney White – leaves room for the food to shine.

619 West Randolph Street, 60661
+1 312 715 0708
blackbirdrestaurant.com

⑫
Lula Café, Logan Square
Firm favourite

Since opening in 1999, Lula Café has anchored Logan Square's dining scene with its ever-changing all-day menu, thoughtful drinks list and cult-favourite brunch. "Lula is built on the foundation of the farm-to-table movement but we consistently challenge ourselves to push the boundaries of what that philosophy can mean," says owner Jason Hammel.

That means dishes such as fried Jerusalem artichokes with charred Chinese broccoli and lamb meatballs with Parisienne gnocchi and grapes. If you're only in town for one night, we suggest you head here – oh, and on Mondays there's a $45 prix-fixe dinner.

2537 North Kedzie Boulevard, 60647
+1 773 489 9554
lulacafe.com

Lunch
Perfect pit-stops

①
Cà Phê Dá, Pilsen
Vietnam café culture

Located next to sister restaurant HaiSous, Cà Phê Dá is a celebration of Vietnamese coffee and street food (such as banh mi and *pho gà*, a chicken and rice noodle soup), as well as delectable pastries such as the pandan brioche with coconut jam.

"Vietnam is the second-largest coffee producer after Brazil and my extended family is one of those roasters," says chef Thai Dang, who co-owns the space with his wife, Danielle. "We wanted not only to educate Chicago on Vietnam's coffee and roadside street-food culture but also to create a welcoming communal space for the neighbourhood."
1800 1/2 South Carpenter Street, 60608
+1 773 999 1800
caphedachi.com

Must-try
Cheeseburger from
Au Cheval, West Loop
With two thin patties, melted American cheese, a slather of Dijonnaise and homemade pickles, the cheeseburger at Au Cheval is perfection in a toasted bun. Add a fried egg or bacon if you want to take it one step further.
auchevalchicago.com

②
Same Day Café, Logan Square
Nice and cheesy

This airy all-day café is ideal for a quick lunch, with in-house sodas and made-to-order sandwiches to enjoy either at your table or the plant-peppered counter. The city's best grilled cheese comprises cheddar and smoked gouda served in rosemary bread; you can add bacon, roasted cherry tomatoes or rocket but you hardly need it.

Other sandwiches include a BLT with Sriracha bacon, a scrambled-egg biscuit with red chimichurri and a curried chicken-salad sandwich with almonds and dates. The homemade sodas range from coffee to Michigan tart cherry.
2651 North Kedzie Avenue, 60647
+1 773 342 7040
samedaycafe.com

3

Dove's Luncheonette, Wicker Park
Tex-Mex with a twist

Mexican and Southern food converge at Dove's Luncheonette, which turns out plates such as a sweetcorn tamale with country ham and a chicken-fried chicken dish (yes, you heard that right) with chorizo verde gravy. All set to a soundtrack of 1960s and 1970s Chicago blues and soul.

The diner setting makes Dove's an easy spot in which to sidle in solo and grab a cocktail from the tequila and mezcal-centric drinks list during happy hour. The jukebox and vintage photos give it an old-school vibe but the food is decidedly modern.

1545 North Damen Avenue, 60622

+1 773 645 4060
doveschicago.com

④

Lost Larson, Andersonville
Swede success

Bobby Schaffer (*pictured*)
honours his Swedish heritage
and the history of the
Andersonville neighbourhood
with this light-filled bakery-
cum-café. Lost Larson is
devoted to Swedish-inflected
dishes such as open-
faced sandwiches stacked
with pickled herring and
lingonberry jam or smoked
ham with dill havarti (a Danish
cheese), lingonberry-almond
cake dusted with powdered
sugar, and limpa (a kind of
rye) bread with fennel and
star anise.

The pastry counter is
a wonder, with croissants
laced with cardamom, lemon
tarts with crowns of toasted
meringue and crumbly savoury
scones. Take home a loaf of
bread made with grains milled
on-site – the flavours range
from traditional wholewheat
to pumpkin seed and kelp.
5318 North Clark Street, 60640
+ 1 773 944 0587
lostlarson.com

⑤
Manny's Deli, South Loop
No-frills classic

When you arrive at this legendary South Loop deli and restaurant, grab a tray and load it up with whatever old-school dish takes your fancy: hearty meatloaf, chicken potpie or a hot turkey dinner. Next, head to any free table in the cafeteria-style dining room and tuck in.

Since 1942, the family-owned Manny's has been serving homely dishes alongside Jewish favourites such as pastrami sandwiches overflowing with meat, melty Reubens, crispy potato pancakes and chopped liver – and the crowds keep on coming.
1141 South Jefferson Street, 60607
+1 312 939 2855
mannysdeli.com

⑥
Marisol, Streeterville
Artful eating

Housed in the Museum of Contemporary Art (*see page 91*), Marisol is a restaurant from chef Jason Hammel of Lula Café (*see page 33*). "The restaurant reimagines the relationship between food, art and design in an immersive art environment," he says. "We've created a menu that rotates with the seasons, filled with imaginative and contemporary flavours inspired by artistic surroundings."

Marisol serves lunch and dinner and also features a coffee shop and bar. A great place to refuel over oysters with grilled lemon or fried quail with cashew butter and smoked-date honey.
205 East Pearson Street, 60611
+1 312 799 3599
marisolchicago.com

Fried-chicken feasts

01 Honey Butter Fried Chicken, Avondale: Slathering the honey butter directly onto the fried chicken at Josh Kulp and Christine Cikowski's fried-chicken temple gives it a rich salty-sweet flavour that melts into the crispy skin. The menu includes whole pieces, chicken strips and towering sandwiches such as the OG, with slaw and candied jalapeño mayo. *honeybutter.com*

02 The Roost Carolina Kitchen, various locations: For Southern-style fried-chicken sandwiches – yes, that includes the fiery hot Nashville – you can't beat The Roost, where juicy fried chicken with a perfectly crunchy coating comes on buttery biscuits with toppings such as pickles, 'slaw or sharp cheddar. Alternatively, try the fried-chicken tacos or classic bone-in chicken with sides. *theroostcarolinakitchen.com*

03 Ina Mae Tavern & Packaged Goods, Wicker Park: New Orleans native Brian Jupiter is Chicago's go-to guy for Southern classics and those include his fried chicken, available in white or dark meat and served with a flaky biscuit and honey. The coating is craggy, crispy and perfectly seasoned, shattering satisfyingly when you take a bite. *inamaetavern.com*

Top tacos

01 Mi Tocaya Antojeria, Logan Square: Acclaimed chef Diana Dávila draws on her Mexican heritage to create tacos including the vegetarian *milpa*, with charred butternut squash, chillies, beans and corn crema. The meaty *campechano*, with *cochinita* (slow-roasted pork), chorizo and *carne asada* (grilled and sliced beef), brings the heat.
mitocaya.com

02 Carnitas Uruapan, Lower West Side: As the name implies, the family-owned Carnitas Uruapan is all about the *carnitas* (luscious slow-cooked pork), which you order by the taco or the pound. Pair a taco with a side of crispy *chicharrones* (fried pork skin).
carnitasuruapanchi.com

03 Antique Taco, various locations: There are three locations of Rick Ortiz's Antique Taco: Wicker Park, Bridgeport and the Loop. Visit them all to try the different fillings, from mushrooms with *guajillo* (chilli) purée to smoked brisket with onions.
antiquetaco.com

04 Cruz Blanca Brewery & Taquería, West Loop: Celebrity chef Rick Bayless focuses on tacos at his lively brewery, where you can order build-your-own taco plates with meats, salsas and sides, or composed tacos such as chopped lamb with crispy cheese and caramelised onion.
rickbayless.com/ restaurants/cerveceria-cruz-blanca

Brunch
Places to linger

❶ Baker Miller, Lincoln Square
Morning munchies

Baked goods are the name of the game at Baker Miller, the café where Dave (*pictured*) and Megan Miller offer their delicious takes on morning favourites. Biscuits stuffed with egg custard, avocado toast adorned with radishes and sourdough French toast accented with seasonal jams sit on the menu alongside grits and grain bowls.

The "famous" oatmeal earns that often overstated moniker: it's the creamiest version you'll have ever had and comes with cultured cream, cinnamon-sugar pecans and a dollop of jam. Grab a bag of pastries (in particular the gooey cinnamon buns) on the way out.
4655 North Lincoln Avenue, 60625
+1 773 654 3610
bakermillerchicago.com

Pie's the limit

When pie cravings strike, Bang Bang Pie & Biscuits delivers sweet and savoury options such as a Buffalo chicken potpie. Bonus: the buttery biscuit sandwiches, with fillings such as candied bacon and pimento cheese, are some of the city's best breakfast fare.
bangbangpie.com

② Bad Hunter, West Loop
Light and bright

This is the place to come if you fancy a lighter brunch. The space is bright and airy, much like chef Dan Snowden's vegetable-focused dishes. Expect to find a freekeh bowl with grilled market vegetables, za'atar and a soft-boiled egg; tempura sweet potato with coconut yoghurt, harissa and pistachio dukkah; and a vegetarian burger in a brioche bun with cheddar, mustard aioli and tomato jam.

The wine list is natural and Emily Spurlin's whimsical pastries include everything from carrot-and-coconut cinnamon rolls to parsnip cake with poached pears and hazelnut.
802 West Randolph Street, 60607
+1 312 265 1745
badhunter.com

③ Lou Mitchell's, West Loop
Start the day the old school way

Not much has changed at Lou Mitchell's over the years – and that's a good thing, since the busy diner has been churning out classic dishes since 1923. The restaurant is open for both breakfast and lunch, with fluffy pancakes and waffles with whipped butter, freshly made hash browns and stuffed omelettes anchoring the morning menu.

Come lunch, there's a variety of burgers and sandwiches, plus daily specials such as turkey dinners, all in hearty portions. If there's a wait (and there likely will be), don't worry – staff will greet you with doughnut holes and Milk Duds.
565 West Jackson Boulevard, 60661
+1 312 939 3111
loumitchells.com

④ Longman & Eagle, Logan Square
Rise and imbibe

Part cosy hotel (*see page 22*), part lively tavern, Longman & Eagle is a popular Logan Square haunt that opens daily for breakfast. Chef Maxwell Robbins' morning menu ranges from the simple and satisfying (potato-and-egg breakfast burrito or French omelette) to the more elaborate (*elotes* Benedict with sour-cream hollandaise or challah French toast with whipped hot-chocolate butter.)

On the weekend there's a changing list of fresh doughnuts and, if you have a leisurely day ahead, you should try the Bloody Mary or extensive whiskey offerings.
2657 North Kedzie Avenue, 60647
+1 773 276 7110
longmanandeagle.com

⑤

The Allis, West Loop
House special

The soaring ceilings and
glittering chandeliers create
a striking backdrop at this
all-day restaurant at Soho
House (*see page 18*), which
is open to non-members.
Choose between classic western
dishes such as homemade
granola with Greek yoghurt
and berries; the smoked-
salmon bagel with tomato,
cucumber, capers and cream
cheese; or the avocado toast
topped with hard-boiled eggs,
basil, lemon and a sprinkling
of chilli.

Sink into a sofa for a
leisurely bite or join the
freelancers at the communal
table, tapping away at their
keyboards over coffee. There
are magazines and newspapers
on offer, the people-watching
is prime and the walls are
hung with artwork by the
likes of Damien Hirst.
*113-125 North Green Street,
60607
+1 312 521 8000
theallis.com*

Big Jones, Andersonville
Southern hospitality

A visit to Big Jones is akin to taking a quick jaunt to the southern states. Chef and co-owner Paul Fehribach (*pictured*) offers a taste of the region's finest cuisine and ingredients, from a Louisiana crayfish omelette to Alabama catfish and grits.

He also draws from historic recipes, with the brunch menu including a colonial-era cornbread and a Big Jones Benedict with house-cured and smoked ham cooked gently in cream. The cocktails too take inspiration from the rich drinking traditions of New Orleans, Savannah and Charleston: we recommend the Sazerac or the Chatham Artillery Punch.
5347 North Clark Street, 60640
+1 773 275 5725
bigjoneschicago.com

Must-try
Mr G from JP Graziano
Grocery Co, West Loop
The speciality sandwich at this Italian grocery has a lot going on (layers of provolone, hot *soppressata*, prosciutto and salami accented with truffle mustard, balsamic vinaigrette, hot oil, red-wine vinegar and more) but it's a beautifully balanced construction.
jpgraziano.com

Coffee and sweet treats
Brews and bites

①

Four Letter Word,
Logan Square
Swear by it

This single-origin-focused
coffee shop and roaster opened
on Burgazada island (off the
coast of Istanbul) in 2014 and
two years later, with two of the
three owners based in Chicago,
began roasting beans stateside
at The Plant (*see page 45*). In
2018, it added this outpost
in Logan Square.

Served alongside pour-overs,
espresso, drip and Turkish
coffee are pastries baked at
the neighbouring Cellar Door
Provisions. The light-filled,
airy space has just a handful of
tables, a long brick coffee bar
and a clear focus on design,
with distinctive light fixtures
and art books for your perusal.
*3022 West Diversey Avenue,
60647
+1 773 360 8932
4lwcoffee.com*

② Metric Coffee, Near West Side
Serious about beans

There's just a handful of seats at Metric Coffee, established in 2013 by Darko Arandjelovic (founder of Caffe Streets in Wicker Park) and Xavier Alexander (former roasting manager at nearby Intelligentsia). Together the pair roast beans – sourced from the likes of Ethiopia, Kenya, Peru and Honduras – on-site with a 1960s German machine.

Swing by the Fulton Market café for a cup of coffee, cold-pressed juices and pastries from Chicago bakeries Hewn and Spilt Milk – or simply to pick up a pack of ground beans to go. There are also coffee-brewing workshops; register online in advance.
2021 West Fulton Street, Suite K-101B, 60612
+1 312 982 2196
metriccoffee.com

Ice, ice, baby

Pretty Cool Ice Cream will remind you why you chased after the ice-cream van as a child. Pastry chef Dana Cree serves creative ice lollies such as coffee pretzel toffee and banana *horchata* (a creamy rice-and-almond concoction). *prettycoolicecream.com*

③ Loba Pastry + Coffee, Lakeview
In for a treat

Valeria Taylor (*pictured*) has a knack for flavour combinations, which means her squeeze of a coffee shop in Lakeview is packed with sweet and savoury treats. The ever-changing menu features delights such as a pepita crunch bar topped with honey-caramelised nuts and caramel-cherry monkey bread.

The coffees include a latte sweetened with violet-flower syrup and an Arcadian latte, Taylor's take on a Turkish coffee. You can also go simple with a single-origin espresso and a sourdough muffin (crunchy on the outside, fluffy in the middle).
3422 North Lincoln Avenue, 60657
+1 773 456 9266
lobapastry.com

④
Doughnut Vault, River North
The hole game

Chicago's tastiest doughnuts
come from a tiny shopfront
inside a former bank vault.
There's no seating, just
trays lined with delectable
doughnuts. Choose between
daily offerings such as the
vanilla, the chestnut-glazed
and the buttermilk old-
fashioned, as well as specials
including the Mexican hot-
chocolate cake.
  Doughnut Vault used to
command hours-long lines
but thankfully its sugary snacks
can now be found at other
cafés around town. Having
said that, it's well worth the
wait. Bear in mind it opens at
08.00 and closes when stock
sells out (sometimes by 10.00).
*401 North Franklin Street,
60654
+1 312 285 2830
doughnutvault.com*

⑤
Sawada Coffee, West Loop
Artist at work

Japanese barista and latte-art
champion (really) Hiroshi
Sawada opened his first
US coffee shop in 2015 in
Chicago's former meatpacking
district. Behind the graffiti-
covered façade is an industrial
space dotted with ping-pong
tables and pinball.
  Sawada's signature military
latte mimics camouflage –
with matcha, vanilla, cocoa
powder and espresso – and
a matching doughnut from
Doughnut Vault (*see left*) is
available. The short menu
also includes teas and boozy
steamers – spiked drinks
such as a milk-based Scotch
and a honey drink laced
with almond.
*112 North Green Street, 60607
+1 312 754 0431
sawadacoffee.com*

Get buzzed

Coffee roaster Intelligentsia is
spreading across the country
but it was born in Chicago,
where it offers its brews at six
cafés. The industrial design of
the Millennium Park location
echoes the nearby sculptures.
intelligentsiacoffee.com

⑥
Gaslight Coffee Roasters,
Logan Square
A good roasting

With metal chairs straight
out of an old-school classroom
and taxidermy hanging on
walls lined with baroque
wallpaper, the long-standing
Gaslight Coffee Roasters is
a fine spot in which to linger
over a silky latte. On weekdays
freelancer types abound while
on the weekend Logan Square
residents catch up with friends
over egg sandwiches, bowls
of spiced tomato soup and
other homely fare.
  Coffee is roasted on-site
with beans sourced from
Guatemala, Ethiopia and
further afield. If you like what
you sip, grab a bag of beans
to go.
*2385 North Milwaukee Avenue,
60647
gaslightcoffeeroasters.com*

Markets
Stall order

①

Green City Market, Lincoln Park
Food fest

Held outside between May and October and indoors at the Peggy Notebaert Nature Museum throughout the rest of the year, the Lincoln Park location of Green City Market draws devoted food lovers and chefs seeking the best vegetables, fruit and other products for their kitchens. Satellite locations of the market are sprouting around the city but the Saturday iteration remains the biggest farmers' market.

Weave your way between stands offering maple syrup, charcuterie, cheese and more – even wood-fired pizzas – all from Illinois and nearby Michigan and Wisconsin. Weekly chef demos invite you to see how the city's top chefs are using the seasonal produce.
Corner of North Clark Street and North Lincoln Avenue
+1 773 880 1266
greencitymarket.org

Go green

On the first Saturday of each month, urban farm and sustainable food business centre The Plant hosts a farmers' market. Drop by to peruse produce grown both by the tenants and other Chicagoans.
plantchicago.org/farmers-market

Drinks
Fine imbibing

① Lost Lake, Logan Square
Paradise found

This vibrant bar is all about the tropical decor and tiki cocktails. Bartender Paul McGee and co-owner Shelby Allison have created a beautiful den with banana leaf-print wallpaper, bamboo decor and a smiling team of bartenders in Hawaiian shirts.

Hop on a stool and ask for one of their perfectly balanced cocktails. The banana daiquiri – featuring Jamaican, Trinidadian and spiced rum – has a banana dolphin leaping out of the glass.
3154 West Diversey Avenue, 60647
+1 773 293 6048
lostlaketiki.com

② Sportsman's Club, Humboldt Park
Drinking den

Sportsman's Club is a bar for all seasons. The taxidermy deer heads lining the slender space and the comfortable booths contribute to a cosy feeling, while the back windows open out onto a big patio that hosts summer barbecues with some of the best chefs in town.

Four cocktails are offered each day, along with wine and craft beer. Or you can order a round of house amaro shots, served in chilled shot glasses.
948 North Western Avenue, 60622
+1 872 206 8054
drinkingandgathering.com

③ Income Tax, Edgewater
Wine and dine

Located in the northern neighbourhood of Edgewater, this sharply designed, low-lit bar and restaurant features a wine list that's geared towards Old World producers.

Pull up a seat at the marble bar and ask for a glass of red or peruse the menu of lesser-known cocktails (try the cider-based Stone Fence, spiked with armagnac), plus the vermouth, brandy, cider and beer lists. A European-focused dinner menu from chef Ellison Park will keep you sated.
5959 North Broadway, 60660
+1 773 897 9165
incometaxbar.com

④
Red & White Wine Bar,
Bucktown
Glass act

In 2018, a decade after Red
& White Wines opened in
Bucktown, the sharp little
shop opened an equally sharp
bar next door. It offers the
same natural wines by the
glass or bottle, as well as a
concise menu of cheese and
charcuterie plus a few small
plates and mains.

The by-the-glass list is
short and sweet and the staff
will talk and taste you through
as many as you want until you
find the perfect glass.
*1861 North Milwaukee Avenue,
60647*
+1 773 486 4769
redandwhitewineschicago.com

⑤
Parson's Chicken & Fish,
Logan Square
The great outdoors

Chicagoans love a good patio
and Parson's has one of the
best in the city. With a sea of
picnic tables, bench seating
and a ping-pong table, this
is somewhere to spend a
low-key summer evening.

There are also plenty of
tables indoors come winter
and the Negroni slushy is
delicious whatever the season.
Local beers and crowd-
pleasing cocktails work well
with grilled or fried chicken
or a fried-fish sandwich.
*2952 West Armitage Avenue,
60647*
+1 773 384 3333
parsonschickenandfish.com

6
The Loyalist, West Loop
Classy cocktails

Tucked underneath John
and Karen Shields' fine-
dining restaurant Smyth is
The Loyalist, known for
its well-made cocktails and
killer burger. The bar's Old
Fashioned is an elegant
variation on the classic, with
maple and a dash of amaro
for a hint of bitterness, while
other cocktails feature seasonal
ingredients such as birch,
charred apples and gooseberry.

A couple of beers clock in
at $4 here so you can drink
on the cheap while indulging
in devilled eggs with smoked
salmon, an aged rib eye
drizzled with brown butter
or the Loyalist cheeseburger,
topped with a mass of onions,
pickles and American cheese.
177 North Ada Street, 60607
+1 773 913 3774
smythandtheloyalist.com

Late-night eats
———
After a night out, swing by
The Wiener's Circle for char
(grilled) dogs, burgers and
freshly cut fries with tangy
cheese. Place your order with
the staff at the counter and
snag a picnic table – it's not
fancy but it's a classic late-
night Chicago custom.
wienercircle.net

⑦
Estereo, Logan Square
Night and day

As the neon sign on the wall proclaims, Estereo is an all-day bar. Drop by in the afternoon for a coffee or come in the evening for drinks made with Latin spirits such as mezcal, tequila, cachaça and pisco. When night falls, live DJs set up in the corner.

Bartender Michael Rubel has assembled an impressive spirits list and the cocktails are indebted to local produce. In summer the windows roll up to let in the breeze.
2450 North Milwaukee Avenue, 60647
+1 773 360 8363
estereochicago.com

⑧
Cindy's, The Loop
High life

The sweeping views from the outdoor patio at Cindy's, the rooftop bar on the 13th floor of the Chicago Athletic Association Hotel (*see page 25*), take in Millennium Park, Lake Michigan, Cloud Gate and a whole load of dazzling architecture in the Loop. But crowds aren't queuing up for the vista alone: the cocktails are exceptional, biodynamic wines and Midwest beers are available and the comfort food is designed for sharing. Also open for brunch and lunch.
12 South Michigan Avenue, 60603
+1 312 792 3502
cindysrooftop.com

⑨
Scofflaw, Logan Square
Cocktails and cookies

Gin is the main focus at this dark and broody cocktail bar where the drinks menu changes every three months but always includes a swizzle that matches the season. Sample gins from around the world or try one in a tiny 'Tini, a miniature martini.

The drinks list includes a glossary of cocktails and there's a menu of small plates. At midnight fresh-baked chocolate-chip cookies are handed out – a reason to stay.
3201 West Armitage Avenue, 60647
+1 773 252 9700
scofflawchicago.com

Retail
—— Shop talk

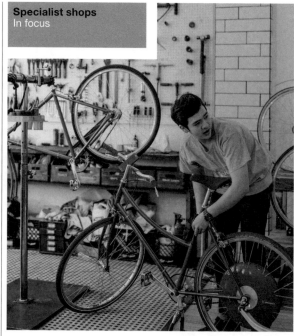

Sitting pretty between the US's sartorially aware east and west coasts, the Midwest has it all: family-run bookshops, luxury fashion houses and out-of-town malls. Here we stick to the city proper, mostly steer clear of Michigan Avenue (Chicago's version of Fifth Avenue or Rodeo Drive) and focus on standalone shops you won't find anywhere else.

Chicago is fairly affordable – at least in comparison to New York or Los Angeles – and as such small businesses have the chance to thrive. Pop in and out of the shops on the following pages and you'll meet many owners who were born and raised nearby.

There are independent retailers across the city, from the art supplies and bookbinding shops of Andersonville to the fashion boutiques north of the Loop and the concept stores cropping up in artsy enclaves such as Bucktown and Wicker Park. Chicago is big on homeware, with dozens of mid-century modern furniture shops, and it's also not short of places to pick up a record or two.

1

Heritage Bicycles General
Store, Lakeview
Wheel deal

The general store of Heritage Bicycles (which also has coffee shops in Uptown) is on the minimalist side, with a black-and-white palette and plenty of old-growth wood. Customers come for the vintage-inspired, handmade bicycles or the pastries and freshly brewed coffee – or all of the above.

Owner Michael Salvatore stumbled upon the space when it was even more pared back – in fact, it was papered-up and empty. "Everyone thought I was crazy," he says. "This was a dead area where nothing survived and no one shopped." He ignored the warning signs, opening in 2012, and six years later expanded next door.
2959 North Lincoln Avenue, 60657
+1 773 245 3005
heritagebicycles.com

②
Martha Mae, Andersonville
Form and function

Jean Cate (*pictured*) moved from southern California to the city in 2008 to study at the School of the Art Institute of Chicago. "After graduating I wanted to dive straight into another project," she says – and she did, setting up her light-filled shop for art supplies and everyday tools in 2016.

Cate makes the paintings, etchings and drawings that line the walls, as well as some of the ceramic work. The maple and granite shelves are stocked with pieces by local makers such as Christie Chapin, plus Cate's favourite international brands including Taiwan-based Tools to Liveby. "I want to help people find beautiful, functional things," she adds.

5407 North Clark Street, 60640
+ 1 872 806 0988
marthamae.info

Greer, Lincoln Park
Take note

Everybody loves a stationery shop and this one, located in the old horse stables of Saint Vincent de Paul Parish, is no exception. Former advertising executive Chandra Greer (*pictured*) founded the shop in 2007 and lives just a few blocks away with her family.

Alongside stationery and desk supplies from international names such as Belgium's Crown Mill, Germany's Dux, Japan's Postalco and France's Calepino, you'll find vintage items Greer has stumbled upon over the years: antique card catalogues; a counter salvaged from a library in Knoxville, Tennessee; and a 1930s postbox from a New York apartment building. "I'm passionate about preserving the functional beauty of an era when there was almost a worshipful approach to craftsmanship," says Greer.

1013 West Webster Avenue, 60614
+1 312 337 8000
greerchicago.com

④
Bari Zaki Studio, North Center
By the book

One in a row of like-minded
makers on North Lincoln
Avenue, Bari Zaki (*pictured*)
– the daughter of a printer
– opened her bookbinding
studio and stationery shop in
2015, having run a small space
in a neighbourhood nearby
for 20 years. Zaki teaches
bookbinding and box-making
workshops twice a month while
guest instructors offer lettering
and drawing classes.
 The airy stop-in is dotted
with blank books, writing and
bookbinding tools, and plenty
of notepads. There's also an
ever-expanding installation
of postcards from around the
world, and the author Audrey
Niffenegger designed the shop
logo back in 1992.
3858 North Lincoln Avenue, 60613
+1 773 294 7766
barizaki.com

⑤
Merz Apothecary,
Lincoln Square
Potions and lotions

Leaded-glass windows with
gold-leaf and hand-painted
signage, custom woodwork,
tin ceilings and twinkling
chandeliers: step into this
family-run pharmacy and,
clichéd as it might sound,
you'll feel as if you've been
transported to a traditional
apothecary in 1800s Vienna.
 Chicago-based Peter Merz
founded a small pharmacy
focused on herbal remedies
in 1875 and, after being
purchased by Abdul Qaiyum
in 1972, the business expanded
and moved to its current
location. Choose between
Santa Maria Novella soaps,
Byredo fragrances and Dr
Hauschka skincare before
nipping next door to the more
modern The Shops at Merz,
featuring men's grooming
specialist Q Brothers.
4716 North Lincoln Avenue,
60625
+1 773 989 0900
merzapothecary.com

(6)
Field & Florist, Wicker Park
Garden variety

Field & Florist operated as a
flower farm and design studio
for five years before opening
this petite bricks-and-mortar
outpost in 2017. Tucked
away on the lower floor of an
Italianate-style building erected
in 1891, the shop is a slice of
calm on busy Division Street.
    Co-founders Heidi Joynt and
Molly Kobelt (*pictured, Joynt on
left*) produce and arrange cut
flowers of the highest quality.
Alongside the dahlias, daffodils
and lisianthuses sustainably
grown on their farm in Harbor
Country, southwest Michigan,
they also offer homeware and
lifestyle items such as skincare
from Malin+Goetz, Regime
des Fleurs fragrances and Casa
Bosques chocolates.
1908 West Division Street, 60622
+1 773 698 7491
fieldandflorist.com

Bottled it
───

Bottles & Cans on North
Lincoln Avenue is packed with
local and international craft
beers, ciders, wines and spirits.
Owners Joe and Carly Katz
set up shop in North Center in
2012 and have been serving
the neighbourhood ever since.
bottlesandcanschicago.com

Field Notes, West Loop
Launching pads

This world-famous stationery brand came about when former design consultant Aaron Draplin made a small run of notebooks by hand and gave them to friends as gifts. One of the recipients was Jim Coudal, who called Draplin and suggested there might be a business there. A decade or so later and the brand sells millions of products a year.

Drop by this industrial-style space in the West Loop to peruse Field Notes' Midwest HQ and studio, as well as the latest offerings in its shop.
401 North Racine Avenue, 60642
+1 312 243 1107
fieldnotesbrand.com

Asrai Garden, Wicker Park
Plant life

Elizabeth Cronin grew up in Wicker Park so when she decided to open a flower shop in 1999, aged just 23, there was no question about the location. "This is the neighbourhood where my parents worked and met and where I spent most of my high-school days," she says.

Housed in the historic Flat Iron building, Asrai Garden is a small, dimly lit shop with an inky-black backdrop and a small section of wallpaper stamped with poppies and bats. Flowers from both down the road and all over the world are displayed alongside fragrances, crystals, jewellery and taxidermy. In late 2018, Cronin opened a second space in the Ace Hotel (*see page 19*).
1935 West North Avenue, 60622
+1 773 782 0680
asraigarden.com

Books and records
Read up and listen in

Sandmeyer's Bookstore, South Loop
Reading recommendations

Former librarians Ellen and Ulrich Sandmeyer were among the first intrepid retailers to set up shop in the city's historic Printers Row district. In 1982 they opened their bookshop in a former bindery from the 19th century, retaining the original wooden floorboards and brick walls. The heavy equipment was replaced with many shelves, which are now stacked with everything from literary fiction and travel guides to children's stories.
714 South Dearborn Street, 60605
+1 312 922 2104
sandmeyersbookstore.com

②

The Dial Bookshop, The Loop
Literary legacy

The Fine Arts Building has a long literary history: two 20th-century journals were published here; Frank Lloyd Wright designed an on-site bookshop and had an office upstairs; and *The Wizard of Oz* was penned and illustrated on the premises. Today, Mary Gibbons and Aaron Lippelt (*pictured*) run The Dial Bookshop on the second floor.

Books sit on shelves made from 100-year-old bleacher wood sourced from a nearby basketball gym. The focus is on contemporary titles but you'll also find vintage and rare tomes, plus small-press publications. "Our collection is curated primarily by customer requests," says Gibbons.
410 South Michigan Avenue, Suite 210, 60605
dialbookshop.com

Sister shop
———
Two years before they opened The Dial Bookshop in 2017, Gibbons and Lippelt established Pilsen Community Books. As well as offering shelves bursting with new and used books, the shop provides reading material for students and teachers.
pilsencommunitybooks.org

③ Hyde Park Records, Hyde Park
Hitting the high notes

This treasure trove of vinyl is a must for any music lover wanting to take home a slice of Chicago's sound. Here you'll find an abundance of tunes by the jazz and blues artists the city is famous for: Muddy Waters, Herbie Hancock, Mavis Staples and many more.

Owner Alexis Bouteville founded Hyde Park Records in 2011 when he took over and renamed the neighbourhood's existing record shop, Second Hand Tunes. There's a bit of everything but the focus is on jazz, blues, funk and soul.
*1377 East 53rd Street, 60615
+1 773 288 6588
hydeparkrecords.com*

Homeware
In the house

① South Loop Loft, River West
All in one

This two-storey homeware shop is a little like an art gallery – just with less blank space. A monochrome backdrop (and a whopping custom-made chandelier) lets the very many objects, works of art and pieces of furniture shine.

Owner Beth Berke (*pictured, on right*), who started her career as a social worker and has spent time as an aid worker in Afghanistan, travels across the world seeking one-off items that span several eras and styles. The items on offer range from mid-century modern Gio Ponti chairs and cushy Thayer Coggin 1980s sectional sofas to reed mats from Mauritania and jewellery from markets in Mexico City. "I don't limit myself to one specific genre," says Berke. "I just buy what I love."
*685 North Milwaukee Avenue, 60642
+1 312 291 8479
thesouthlooploft.com*

2

Neybir, West Town
Get involved

In case you're wondering, the name of this West Town shop is pronounced like "neighbour". Founded by interior designer turned painter Kimberly Postma in 2015, it offers original artwork, modern pieces and vintage homeware.

Alongside Postma's own paintings you'll find woodwork by Lou Robinson, pottery by Polly Yates, jewellery by Julie Crosson, furniture by Kendall Karmanian and much more, including terrariums and pot plants. "I want to spark creativity and provide home and lifestyle goods that represent the past, present and future," says Postma, who also hosts creative workshops.

2246 West Grand Avenue, 60612
+1 312 600 6306
neybir.com

③
Sprout Home Kitchen
& Table, West Town
Inside out

In 2003, Tara Heibel opened
Sprout Home – a plant and
garden shop – on Damen
Avenue and in 2016 Sprout
Home Kitchen & Table sprang
up opposite. Drop by the
former to pick up hard-to-
find plants and flowers then
nip across to the tin-ceilinged
Kitchen & Table (*pictured*) for
well-designed homeware and
accessories. "We offer things
you'll want to live with for a
long time, along with advice as
to how your plants can do the
same," says Heibel.
744 North Damen Avenue, 60622
+1 312 226 9650
sprouthome.com

④
Velvet Goldmine,
Ukrainian Village
Source material

The selection of mid-century
modern design here changes
daily, depending on what
owners Jon Gorske and
Kurt Niesman have sourced
recently. The focus is on
Scandinavian and US design,
with pieces by the likes of
George Mulhauser, Kofod-
Larsen and Adrian Pearsall.
    "On average we drive
about 800 to 1,000 miles a
week," says Gorske, who
studied art and design
before segueing into retail.
"The demand for vintage in
Chicago is insatiable." The pair
opened their shop in a former
recording studio in 2016;
don't miss Rainbo Club, one
of the city's oldest dive bars,
at the back of the building.
2001 West Division Street, 60622
+1 312 493 1660

More mid-century modern

01 Circa Modern, East
    Village: You know you're
    in good hands when a
    furniture shop is run by
    a former architect and
    a former gallerist. Call
    ahead if you're interested
    in a specific piece on the
    website so the owners
    can transfer it from
    warehouse to shop.
    circamodern.com

02 Dial M for Modern,
    Logan Square: Timothy
    Burkhart sources mainly
    US and Danish designs
    for his shop dedicated to
    vintage and mid-century
    modern pieces.
    dialmformodern.com

03 Modern Times, West
    Town: Since opening in
    1991, Martha Torno and
    Tom Clark's Modern
    Times has offered visitors
    a discerning range of mid-
    century furniture, lighting,
    jewellery and more.
    moderntimeschicago.com

04 Mint Home, Lincoln
    Square: Alongside
    vintage pieces of furniture
    – some reclaimed, others
    sold as is – Mint Home
    features household
    items made by artists
    and designers based
    in Chicago and further
    afield in the US.
    minthomechicago.com

Household name
—
With nearly 30 shops –
and some 1,000 wholesale
locations – around the world,
potter and designer Jonathan
Adler is a well-known entity
when it comes to homeware.
Drop by his well-stocked shop
in River North for everything
from bedding to bookends.
jonathanadler.com

Concept stores
Bright ideas

Tusk, Logan Square
Different guises

Drop by on any given day
and Tusk might be a boutique,
a gallery, a supper club or a
stage for shows and readings.
"It's a mix of things I've found
and love," says Mary Eleanor
Wallace (*pictured*), who comes
from a family of collectors.

Wallace moved to Chicago in
2007 to be a nurse and six years
later opened Tusk in an old deli
– look out for the dumbwaiter.
The shop is stocked with small
brands and artist collaborations,
as well as one-off pieces by
Wallace and her friends.
*3205 West Armitage Avenue,
60647*
+1 423 903 7093
tuskchicago.com

① Space 519, Streeterville
Shop then eat

Space 519 started life in
2010 in a luxury shopping
centre on Michigan Avenue.
"We literally were space 519
in the building," says Lance
Lawson, a former attorney who
co-founded the shop with his
partner Jim Wetzel. In 2018
they moved to the ground floor
of this 1920s building on East
Chestnut Street and added
The Lunchroom, a 40-seat
restaurant with Breuer chairs
and white marble tables.

On offer are women's
clothes from independent
designers such as Apiece Apart,
accessories discovered on
Lawson and Wetzel's quarterly
trips to Paris, homeware and
books – and much more. "We
want to be a place of discovery
for our clients – somewhere
special they wish to return to,"
says Wetzel.
200 East Chestnut Street, 60611
+1 312 751 1519
space519.com

③

Rider for Life, West Loop
Cool rider

This West Loop shop is chock-a-block with unique pieces by contemporary artists and designers: artwork by Butch Anthony, whose skeletal embroidery stretches across hand-painted replicas of classic paintings; Leslie Baum ceramics; and futuristic lighting by TJ O'Keefe.

Lauren McGrady opened Rider for Life in 2015 after discovering myriad makers on her travels. "I made purchases and lists along the way and ended up with a big enough collection to open my own bazaar," she says.
1115 West Lake Street, 60607
+1 312 243 0464
riderforlife.myshopify.com

④

Eskell, Bucktown
In full swing

After graduating from the Fashion Institute of Technology and spending five years working for independent designers in New York, Kelly Whitesell moved back to Chicago and founded Eskell in 2005. She started off with a clothing line designed together with her then partner Elizabeth Del Castillo but as the shape of the fashion industry shifted so too did her interests.

"I wanted more than just clothes," says Whitesell, who began expanding her range into homeware and lifestyle goods and today also provides design consultation services. Since 2017, Eskell has been housed in a newly designed building with Belgian tiles at the entrance. As well as the furniture and other pieces on offer, it's an enjoyable place to hang out, complete with a swing and a piano.
2029 North Western Avenue, 60647
+1 773 486 0830
eskell.com

Menswear
Male order

Independence, West Loop
Best foot forward

George Vlagos founded
Oak Street Bootmakers in
2010 and went on to open
Independence, the flagship
retailer for the former, two
years later. Just as the boots
are designed and produced
in the US – using Chicago's
Horween Leather, no less –
the focus at Independence
is on national brands.

"We're not about fashion
and trends," says Vlagos, who
initially set up shop on Oak
Street. In 2019, Independence
moved to a former food and
seed warehouse on Randolph
Street in the West Loop,
kitted out with Vlagos's own
vintage furniture and 19th
and 20th-century hand-knit
rugs. Alongside Oak Street
Bootmakers, expect to find
Engineered Garments, Gitman
Brothers Vintage and, as an
exception to the rule, OrSlow
and Kapital from Japan.
*920 West Randolph Street, 60607
independence-chicago.com*

2 Stock MFG, Near West Side
Hip hangout

"We try to make the shop a
comfortable place to hang out,"
says CEO Jim Snediker, who
co-founded Stock MFG together
with creative director Mike
Morarity (*pictured, on left*) and
head of product Tim Tierney
(*pictured, on right*) in 2012.
They've succeeded: this bricks-
and-timber space in the Kinzie
Industrial Corridor features
antiques, vintage baseball flags
and a restored 1963 AMF pool
table. Most items are made
nearby from Japanese textiles
and North American denim
and canvas.
*2136 West Fulton Street, 60612
+1 312 371 1555
stockmfgco.com*

③
BLVDier, West Loop
Tinker tailor

Zach and Kirsten Uttich founded their tailored-clothing shop – a tiny space that caters to one customer at a time – in 2015. The pair met at university and have backgrounds in the arts: Kirsten is a tap dancer and Zach, though he's been in the clothing business for 10 years, studied theatre.

BLVDier is an abbreviated form of boulevardier, the name for a fashionable man about town in Paris. "Our customers are culturally minded and conscious of how their wardrobe affects their lifestyle," says Zach. Listen to the likes of Smokey Robinson as you're fitted for a made-to-measure suit crafted from Italian and English fabrics.
211 North Green Street, 60607
+1 312 632 0482
blvdier.com

Womenswear
Feminine touch

①
Ikram, River North
Ladies in red

Ikram Goldman, the inimitable founder of this wild and wacky fashion boutique, was the former stylist of Michelle Obama – need we say more? Ok then. Behind the glossy red façade on East Huron Street is not only an opulent shop but also a café and a gallery.

Expect to find clothes, shoes, bags and jewellery by designers who aren't stocked elsewhere in the city, as well as one-of-a-kind pieces by the world's industry leaders, from Chanel and Céline to Lanvin and Manolo Blahnik. Dotted among these off-the-runway items are vintage clothes and accessories, all chosen by Goldman herself.
15 East Huron Street, 60611
+1 312 587 1000
ikram.com

2
Union Handmade, North Center
Meet the makers

"We're a community of like-minded shopkeepers," says Leigh Deleonardo, who started out making clothes for her Barbie and honed her skills at the School of the Art Institute of Chicago. The shop she founded in 2013 with her husband, Greg Walker, sits alongside four retail spaces built in the 1920s and designed by Robert Rud, who owns Hawthorne (three doors down).

Union Handmade itself is a collaborative project, with six clothing designers, three milliners, two jewellers, a knitter, a weaver and a leather-worker – all of whom help cover the rent, work in the shop and fill it with their wares. Deleonardo's own clothing line is sewn by Sui Lan Tong-Chan and features an earthy palette.
3860 North Lincoln Avenue, 60613
+1 773 348 1400
unionhandmade.com

③
Blake, Near North Side
To the letter

You'll have to ring the bell and wait to be buzzed in before entering this high-end womenswear offering from Marilyn Blaszka and Dominic Marcheschi, both of whom studied fine art. The pair founded the boutique – housed in a historic post office with high ceilings, big windows and lots of natural light – about 30 years ago and it's always evolving.

The open-plan space is brimming with big names – from Balenciaga and Dior to Jil Sander and Saint Laurent – as well as emerging designers near and far, including Molly Goddard. Dries Van Noten fans, walk this way: Blake is the only shop in Chicago that carries the Belgian designer.
212 West Chicago Avenue, 60654
+1 312 202 0047

Milking it

It's worth dropping into Milk Handmade if only to meet owner Hallie Borden's beautiful retired greyhound, Sauvie. This women's boutique opened in Andersonville in 2012 and offers clothing and accessories from independent brands.
milkhandmade.com

④
p.45, Wicker Park
In Tunstall we trust

When Tricia Tunstall (*pictured*) founded p.45 in 1997, the space had a distinctly avant garde feel. "Our racks were part of a big steel structure that curved around the shop and there was a hole in the front that we called the pit," she says. "Now we're all grown up with a minimal feel, white wood and steel racks running along the exposed brick."

Hanging on those racks are timeless pieces by designers from the US and abroad, including Rachel Comey and Ganni. Tunstall and her team are on hand to advise. As one loyal customer says, "If it doesn't look good, Tunstall's staff won't let you buy it."
1643 North Damen Avenue, 60647
+1 773 862 4523
p45.com

Mixed and accessories
Better together

① Gemini, Wicker Park
Twice as nice

Husband-and-wife duo Jena Frey and Joe Lauer (*pictured*) founded the fashion boutique Penelope's in 2002 and 16 years later opened this slightly higher-end sister shop, Gemini, next door. Behind a classic Chicago shopfront erected in 1885 is a light and airy white-walled space with walnut floors and splashes of colour, from geometric rugs by Brooklyn designer Cold Picnic to furniture by Los Angeles-based Amigo Modern.

"We wanted to bring to our neighbourhood a world-class boutique for men and women that blends the best in contemporary fashion and design with heritage collections," says Lauer. French workwear by Vetra and traditional shirts by Portuguese Flannel brush shoulders with playful womenswear by Barcelona-based Paloma Wool and Swedish menswear by Our Legacy. Plus wall hangings, leather bags and many more "Made in Chicago" wares.
1911 West Division Street, 60622
+1 773 394 1034
geminishop.com

② Lab Rabbit Optics, East Village
Look sharp

"I was born and raised in Wisconsin, went to college for a year, got kicked out for being a clown, then got a job in an optical lab," says Coyote DeGroot, owner of Lab Rabbit Optics. He started selling frames and prescription lenses out of his apartment in Wicker Park in 2009 before setting up shop nearby the following year.

Alongside its in-house line – designed in Chicago and handmade in Fukui, Japan – Lab Rabbit Optics stocks emerging brands including Germany-based Reiz and Japanese labels such as Yellows Plus. "You won't find familiar names here," says DeGroot.
1104 North Ashland Avenue, 60622
+1 773 957 4733
labrabbit.com

③
Billy Reid, West Loop
Modern Americana

Alabama-based Billy Reid was the first fashion designer to set up shop on Randolph Street in late 2015. For this Midwest shop, he chose a former distribution centre for butcher paper near Restaurant Row. "Billy likes to be close to the best restaurants," says sales director Jacob Fulton.

The history of both the area and the two-storey building reflects the collection of men's and womenswear. Hanging on brass racks and illuminated by natural light filtering through a large copper-framed window are classic US clothes with a modern twist. Think plaid work shirts, cord trousers, shearling coats and at least one or two snappy suits.

845 West Randolph Street, 60607
+1 312 614 1503
billyreid.com

④
Optimo, The Loop
Hats off

"Great hats have always been part of our culture," says Graham Thompson, who founded Optimo at the age of 22 before beginning a seven-year apprenticeship with the legendary Chicago hatmaker Johnny Tyus. The first downtown Chicago shop cropped up in 2013 and the flagship (*pictured*) opened in the historic Monadnock building three years later.

Wild-fur felt hats appear to float in front of elegant grey walls while hand-woven straw fedoras are separated by a screen of wooden lasts. All of the products are made in Optimo's factory, a century-old fire station redesigned by Chicago-based SOM in 2018.

51 West Jackson Boulevard, 60604
+1 312 922 2999
optimo.com

It's all in the jeans
—
Every pair of jeans sold by former bond trader Rob McMillan's Dearborn Denim is cut and sewn in Chicago; the denim itself comes from one of the oldest mills in the US. Input your measurements online or head to the Hyde Park shop to be fitted in person.
dearborndenim.us

Things we'd buy
—— Chicago's most coveted

It may not be famous as a retail destination but scratch below the surface and you'll discover that Chicago is chock-a-block with independent shops selling products proudly made in the city. Beyond the luxury department stores on Michigan Avenue, there are many family-run stop-ins capitalising on Chicago's manufacturing history and Midwest materials.

We've scoured the streets for the tastiest take-homes, from crunchy peanut butter and yolk-yellow mustard to a bottle of bourbon and a couple of craft pale ales. Look the part with a pair of boots made from the city's famous Horween Leather and a hat shaped by hand in a former fire station.

You can't come to this city of jazz and leave without a record or two – and, while you're at it, make sure you leaf through the literature on offer. Here's a round-up of our favourite "Made in Chicago" items, including a Cubs baseball cap to top it off.

01 Snow & Graham pencils from Greer *greerchicago.com*
02 Chicago edition notebook by Field Notes *fieldnotesbrand.com*
03 Chicago Cubs baseball cap *citywide*
04 Hand-bound notebook and clips by Bari Zaki Studio *barizaki.com*
05 Fridge magnets and Ted Naos Chicago Skyline Series cards from the Art Institute Chicago Museum Shop *shop.artic.edu*
06 Woodland coffee scoop and Christie Chapin ceramics from Martha Mae *marthamae.info*
07 Little Fire Ceramics plates from Sprout Home Kitchen & Table *sprouthome.com*
08 Printer's Row Coffee Co coffee from Sandmeyer's Bookstore *sandmeyersbookstore.com*
09 Co-op Sauce poblano mustard and Nutmeg's peanut butter from Olivia's Market *oliviasmarket.com*
10 RXBAR protein bar from Rapha Cycling Club *rapha.cc*
11 Letherbee gin from Independent Spirits *shop.independentspiritsinc.com*
12 Bourbon by Koval *koval-distillery.com*
13 Cold brew coffee by Limitless *limitlesscoffee.com*
14 Hopewell Brewing and Marz Community Brewing pale ales from Bottles & Cans *bottlesandcanschicago.com*
15 Washbag by Defy *defybags.com*
16 Oleo Soapworks Windy City Barbershop shave soap from Merz Apothecary *merzapothecary.com*
17 Chicago Comb Co comb and leather case from Q Brothers *qbrothers.com*
18 Tatine Rum Vert hand soap from Fleur *fleurchicago.com*
19 Sweet Comb Chicago Propolis mouth spray and body balm from Merz Apothecary *merzapothecary.com*

20 Jamie LaPorta for Ruby
Bohannon scarf from Union
Handmade *unionhandmade.com*
21 Hat by Optimo *optimo.com*
22 Oak Street Bootmakers
boots from Independence
independence-chicago.com
23 Workwear shirt by
Stock MFG *stockmfgco.com*

24 Tote bag by Defy
defybags.com
25 T-shirt by Heritage Bicycles
heritagebicycles.com
26 *Down at Teresa's... Chicago
Blues* from The Dial Bookshop
dialbookshop.com
27 *Chicago Stories* by Michael
Czyzniejewski from Curbside
Books & Records
curbsidesplendor.com

28 Records from Hyde
Park Records
hydeparkrecords.com
29 *The Work of Frank Lloyd
Wright* from The Dial Bookshop
dialbookshop.com
30 Eye of the Sun pyramid
handbag from Gemini
geminishop.com

10 essays
—— The stories of Chicago

The whole 'wise' thing doesn't happen by accident, you know

More than mobsters
The contribution of Chicago

You'd be surprised at the things Chicago has given the world – from scientists and comedians to the identity of a whole musical genre.

by Robert K Elder,
writer

Chicago is in your head and you don't even know it.

The Windy City has made lasting contributions to industry, labour, comedy, the arts, economics and science. It's also added to your vocabulary.

"Skyscraper" was first used in print in the *Chicago Inter-Ocean* newspaper in 1888 to describe the 10-storey Montauk Building. "Jazz" was coined as a term for a music genre in 1915 by the *Chicago Tribune*; originally, it meant "pep" or "energy". And then, of course, there's "laid" (first popularised between 1900 and 1911), now slang for having sexual intercourse. The term had its origins among customers of the famous brothel the Everleigh Club (pronounced "ever-lay"). They would go to "get Everleighed", thus helping to popularise the phrase "get laid". A legendary prostitute at the club? Suzy Poon Tang.

But long before Chicago began to shape the English language, it was an abandoned Jesuit mission (1696 to 1700) in disputed Native American territory. It was only in 1779 that Haitian trader Jean Baptiste Point du Sable established a permanent settlement there, which was the first of the city's many incarnations.

Soldiers and settlers were subsequently driven out of the newly established Fort Dearborn after it burned during the War of 1812. The army returned to rebuild it in 1816, before the city experienced yet another reshuffle in 1871, when the Great Chicago Fire swept through it, killing about 300 citizens and reducing great swathes of the city to ash. A third of the city's 300,000 residents were left homeless by the blaze.

Of course, there was no option but to rebuild; by then Chicago had established itself as a transport hub, with vast railroad links and shipping lanes that connected the Great Lakes to the Gulf of Mexico via the Mississippi River. Within a few short years, Chicago had reconstructed itself almost completely. "It is hopeless for the occasional visitor to try to keep up with Chicago," said Mark Twain in 1883. "She outgrows his prophecies faster than he can make them."

And Twain hadn't even anticipated the World's Columbian Exposition. The 1893 world's fair would give us the Ferris wheel, the zip, Wrigley's chewing gum, Cracker Jack and, most darkly, serial killer Herman Webster Mudgett (also known as HH Holmes). Mudgett was the "devil" in author Erik Larson's 2003 bestseller *The Devil in the White City*, which chronicled the building of the beaux arts fairgrounds and how Mudgett preyed on the expo's visitors.

Crime and corruption were already deeply ingrained. What could you expect of a city that spawned local politicians with names such as "Bathhouse" John Coughlin and Michael "Hinky Dink" Kenna? In the 1920s, Al Capone rose to prominence as Chicago's most powerful gangster and his reputation cast a long, decade-spanning shadow on the city. (Chicago also added "racketeering" to our collective vocabulary.)

Chicago's industrial revolution fostered the labour movement and supported the Great Migration (1916 to 1970) as more than six million African-Americans moved north for better working and living

conditions. More than a few, including blues legend Muddy Waters, would record songs with Chess Records, inspiring everyone from the Rolling Stones to Bonnie Raitt.

As Twain predicted, Chicago's contributions to the world would be too numerous to keep up with. Architect Frank Lloyd Wright, writer Ernest Hemingway and secretary of state Hillary Clinton would all call the Chicago suburbs home. Future president Barack Obama would teach at the University of Chicago, which has produced 98 Nobel laureates and alumni that include philosopher John Dewey, astronomer Carl Sagan and economist Milton Friedman. The university also provided the brainpower and location for the first controlled nuclear chain reaction in 1942, pivotal in the development of the nuclear bomb.

Chicago has a lighter side too. It has been fertile ground for comedy, nurturing the likes of Tina Fey, Bill Murray, John Belushi and Melissa McCarthy. Improv comedy was invented in Chicago (you're welcome and we're sorry) and The Second City and iO Theater discover comedy stars with shocking regularity. The city also launched the careers of novelists such as Saul Bellow, Richard Wright, Nelson Algren and Gillian Flynn. We simply don't have the space to rhapsodise about sports dynasties and music.

It's the place that gave rise to the working-class theatre of David Mamet and the gritty Steppenwolf Theatre; a city where your dreams can come true, with enough luck and tenacity. And that's another Chicago contribution to the national lexicon: "The American Dream". In 1916, the *Chicago Tribune* wrote: "If...the American dream, and the structures which Americans have erected are not worth fighting for to maintain and protect, they were not worth fighting for to establish."

Yes, Chicago has always been in your head; now you know why. — (M)

ABOUT THE WRITER: Robert K Elder is an innovation executive and has written and edited 11 books, including *Hidden Hemingway*.

ESSAY 02

When the lights go down
Chicago's nightlife

You'll be doing yourself a disservice if you don't sample Chicago's after-dark amusements. Here are some highlights.

by Toya Wolfe, writer

Welcome to Chicago! Before we chat about this city's lively music, comedy and theatre scenes, let's be honest: some of this stuff is going to be a little too much for you. And that's ok; there's plenty to choose from. For a good time, you've just got to sift through the myriad options and figure out what you're up for.

Our entertainment spots range from small rooms with hidden entrances to theatres with signs you can read from a block away. If you're after a comedy show to crack you up you'll need to decide how involved you want to be; one troupe relies solely on audience participation while others are fuelled simply by laughter.

Whether you've rolled in solo, with friends or with your partner, there's a taxi, bus or train ready to whisk you

away from that lovely hotel room of yours. So here's my personal list of spots to check out before you, well, check out.

If you're being dragged out of your room reluctantly, I'd suggest two laid-back destinations where you can sip on something and pretend you're still at home. One is Buddy Guy's Legends in the South Loop, named after the rock'n'roll hall-of-famer who has won seven Grammy Awards. It has the essence of a juke joint from the Dirty South, with tonnes of tables and chairs plus enough open space to sway the night away, if you're up for it.

Another low-key affair is Elastic Arts, located on a quiet residential street in Logan Square. You'll feel like you're on a scavenger hunt as you search for the front door. Your reward? A dimly lit, simple space with performances that stretch across jazz, hip-hop, spoken word, electronic and experimental music, dance/movement, puppetry and visual art. Thursday nights are devoted to improvised music; you really are experiencing something fresh here.

"Improvised music removes that pre-composed starting point and asks all of the musicians to compose in the moment," says free-jazz saxophonist Dave Rempis. If you've never tried it, move this place to the top of your list.

Maybe you don't need convincing. Maybe you're asking, "Where's the party?" If so, head to The Promontory in Hyde Park, where you can enjoy afro-fusion, a burlesque show or a themed night out. Subterranean (SubT) in Wicker Park may be a concert hall but it's also a great place to sweat out a day of meetings or work off those slices of deep-dish pizza.

"If you're after a comedy show to crack you up you'll need to decide how involved you want to be; one troupe relies solely on audience participation"

When you're ready for laughs, may I suggest The Neo-Futurists on North Ashland Avenue? The actors perform 30 plays in 60 minutes. The numbers – clamped on a string that runs the length of the stage – are snatched down one at a time. You scream out a number and the loudest mouth gets its way. At the end of each scene you do it all over again, until the 60-minute timer is up. It's raucous and fun.

The other two improv comedy spots, The Second City and iO Theater, boast big-name alumni such as Stephen Colbert, Seth Meyers, Mike Myers, Bill Hader, Dan Aykroyd and Steve Carell – the list goes on.

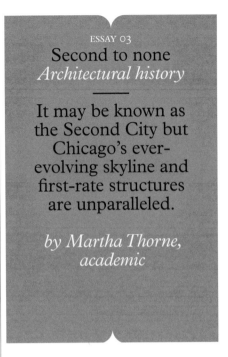

These tickets can sell out before you reach the box office so snap them up in advance.

On the stand-up side there's Up Comedy Club (which offers stand-up, sketch and improv) and Zanies, a short walk away. If your gut and facial muscles can handle it, maybe take in two shows in one night. Zanies, which has three other locations (two in Illinois, one in Nashville), boasts that it's been "sharing laughs since 1978", with "national headliners every night".

Finally, don't miss the Laugh Factory on North Broadway. You'll know that you've come to the right place for jokes: the word "Laugh" is displayed in huge letters, with an electronic awning scrolling bright names and entrance doors painted in pink, gold and turquoise. Keep an eye out for themed evenings, including *Drink Date Laugh* (a great comedy showcase/game show for lovebirds) and *Everyone's a Lawyer*, where three comedians argue their way out of a scenario while you laugh until it hurts.

Well, that's my list. Happy singing, dancing, laughing, chilling and grooving. Snap some photos with your new friends and the talented entertainers who've worked so hard to impress you, post the pictures, then head back to that lovely hotel room; this town can wear you out. — (M)

ABOUT THE WRITER: Toya Wolfe is a fiction writer from Chicago's South Side. Her stories have appeared in publications such as *African Voices* and *Chicago Reader*, and she is the author of the novel, *Landmarks*.

ESSAY 03
Second to none
Architectural history

It may be known as the Second City but Chicago's ever-evolving skyline and first-rate structures are unparalleled.

by Martha Thorne, academic

Chicago may have been branded the nation's Second City but in my eyes it will always be number one.

Just look at its privileged setting: located on the southwest shore of Lake Michigan, with parks and beaches that extend for more than 40km along the shimmering lakefront, creating a natural backdrop that's hard to beat. (Also, if we're going to talk about undeserved nicknames, the moniker the Windy City was originally given to Chicago not because of the strong blasts that blow across the plains and down the avenues but because of its boastful politicians and their overly enthusiastic promotion of the city. In reality, Chicago doesn't even make the list of the 30 windiest cities in the US.)

Perhaps the thing that Chicago really excels at is architecture. The city's skyline is constantly evolving and Chicago has many wonderful spaces beyond the gleaming skyscrapers and the landmark buildings by Frank Lloyd Wright, Louis Sullivan and Mies van der Rohe. There

"The city's skyline is constantly evolving and Chicago has many wonderful spaces beyond the gleaming skyscrapers and landmark buildings"

are real gems to be discovered by those who take the time to dig a little deeper – behind the façades of some of Chicago's best-known buildings, surprises await.

A particular favourite of mine is the InterContinental Hotel on North Michigan Avenue, not far from the famous Tribune Tower. The original building, the south tower, dates back to 1929, when it was built as the Medinah Athletic Club by the Shriners, before becoming a hotel in 1944. The 1920s was a time of great variety and debate surrounding architectural styles, a time when looking back for inspiration from history was in vogue. Here, an eclectic mix of styles came together and was freely interpreted. Egyptian, Assyrian and Greek ornaments adorn the grand ballroom while the indoor swimming pool on the 14th floor nods to southern Spain or northern Africa, with a terracotta fountain of Neptune and palm trees. It's said that Johnny Weissmuller, the original Tarzan, trained here.

You'll find plenty of interesting and inspiring lobbies throughout the Loop if you're willing to explore beyond the imposing thresholds of its buildings. The famous Rookery Building is a treasure: originally created by architects Burnham and Root, it features a glass-ceilinged lobby that was remodelled by Frank Lloyd Wright in 1905.

The art deco marble-and-aluminium lobby of the Board of Trade Building – completed in 1930 – is equally impressive, while the 1987 structure at 190 South LaSalle by Philip Johnson and John Burgee revels in its postmodernism, including a chequerboard marble floor and barrel-vault ceiling accented with gold leaf.

The Art Institute of Chicago is home – in addition to all its famous artwork – to a Tadao Ando-designed gallery built in 1992 that houses Japanese screens. Tucked away within the Asian galleries, the space is intimate and dimly lit, with the result that visitors naturally lower their voices and walk softly upon entering.

Another of the city's destinations that possesses a certain magical quality is the courtyard garden of the Graham Foundation at the Madlener House. The building itself was designed in the early 1900s by architect Richard E Schmidt and designer Hugh MG Garden for a prominent Chicago family. Today the private urban garden situated to the side of the house also serves as an outdoor gallery to showcase Chicago's past, featuring a collection of 19th and 20th-century architectural fragments that have been salvaged from the city's rich history.

So yes, Chicago may well be known as the Second City but if you look a little more closely – especially at its architecture – you'll soon see that this metropolis is second to none. — (M)

ABOUT THE WRITER: Martha Thorne is dean of IE School of Architecture and Design, part of IE University in Madrid. She is also executive director of the Pritzker Architecture Prize, a position she has held since 2005.

ESSAY 04

Portrait of a nation
Grant Wood's 'American Gothic'

Its image of straitlaced country folk has the ability to intrigue and unsettle. What's the subtext of "American Gothic" and what does it tell us about the American people?

by Chloë Ashby, Monocle

Visiting Grant Wood's "American Gothic" (1930) in the Art Institute of Chicago is a little like visiting Leonardo da Vinci's "Mona Lisa" (1503) in the Louvre. Granted (no pun intended), the crowd isn't quite so big but, in the US at least, this orderly double portrait is just as famous – and the expressions of the sitters equally baffling.

Born in 1891 in neighbouring Iowa, Wood spent his early years on the family farm before moving with his mother and siblings to the city of Cedar Rapids. After school he trained as a painter, craftsman and designer, and in the early 1920s travelled to Paris and enrolled at the Académie Julian, where he was inspired by the dappled canvases of the impressionists. A subsequent trip to Munich and time spent among the artwork of 15th and 16th-century German and Flemish masters saw a substantial change to his style. His paintings from then on were highly realistic – semi-stylised – and brimming with crisp details.

Wood reflected, when talking to a journalist in 1940, that upon returning to Iowa after his trips to Europe, he saw "like a revelation, my neighbours in Cedar Rapids, their clothes, their homes, the patterns on their tablecloths and curtains, the tools they used. I suddenly saw all this commonplace stuff as material for art. Wonderful material." It was at this time that he decided to cast himself a regionalist: a wholesome farmer-painter in denim overalls, not dissimilar to those worn by the man with the creased face in "American Gothic".

Wood painted his most famous piece in 1930 and, soon after, it was exhibited and bought by the Art Institute. Here it remains, in Gallery 263 of the American Modern Art wing, perhaps the most popular US painting in history – and certainly the most parodied. Aside from there being something inherently "American" about the work, those two very blank faces allow viewers to see whatever they want to see.

On the one hand, this razor-sharp portrait is a celebration of honourable and hardworking citizens in the US heartland; a salute to those men and women holding steady (and eerily upright) against the hardship of the Great Depression, which swept through the country from 1929 to 1941. The farmer and his daughter – often mistaken for his wife – could be viewed as our very own Adam and Eve (pre-temptation). They pose, pale-faced with pursed lips, in front of a modest farmhouse

with an ecclesiastical façade and that all-important gothic window. Behind them, a bucolic backdrop of a blue sky and green trees. Through the vertical stripes on the farmer's shirt, the white wood panelling on the house and the three prongs of the pitchfork, Wood may be emphasising the upstanding nature of these country folk. But is he?

This straitlaced pair aren't without their flaws: the loose lock of the daughter's hair, a snake-like curl caressing her bare skin; the sinister nature of the pitchfork – this unsmiling man is capable of violence (a nod to the devil?). Those vacant expressions and old-fashioned clothes – the mud-splattered overalls, the earthy-brown pinny. Is Wood toying with us? It's not difficult to read into the scene some satire of small-town life and narrow Midwestern minds.

Stand before the painting in the Art Institute and you'll feel the farmer's unflinching gaze through his small

"This straitlaced pair aren't without their flaws: the loose lock of the daughter's hair, a snake-like curl caressing her bare skin; the sinister nature of the pitchfork – this unsmiling man is capable of violence"

round glasses, shaded by bushy eyebrows. Stand to the right, reading the small white label beyond the wooden frame (the mauve walls in the gallery are suitably morose), and it's hard not to feel uneasy, the object of his daughter's cold stare. Wood modelled her on his sister, Nan, and the farmer on his dentist, Dr Byron McKeeby. The white wooden farmhouse itself still stands in Eldon, a farming town in Iowa. When Wood drove past it in 1930, it was the top window – arched like those he had seen on grand cathedrals in France – that caught his eye.

So what does Wood's painted world tell us about the reality of the "American Dream", then and now? Some 20 years after the phrase first appeared in the *Chicago Tribune*, it was immortalised in writer and historian James Truslow Adams's book *The Epic of America* (1931), just a year after Wood painted his double portrait. It was a "dream" that sought to save the nation, promoting spirituality and prosperity at a time of social and economic upheaval.

It's hard, standing in front of "American Gothic" today, to know whether Wood embraced a similar agenda. It's hard, in light of modern US history and especially in a politically active city such as Chicago (where Barack "Yes We Can" Obama's career gestated), not to read social anxiety and upheaval in the layers of oil paint.

One thing that's easy to do? Look. Pause in front of this painting – by one of the most prominent figures in 20th-century US art – and absorb the scene in front of you. As with the "Mona Lisa", you may not be able to read the minds of the sitters, but that ambiguity may be just the thing to keep your feet firmly rooted. — (M)

ABOUT THE WRITER: Chloë Ashby has a degree in art history and is an associate editor at MONOCLE. Visiting this glum pair in the Art Institute was a highlight of her trip to the Windy City.

ESSAY 05
Packing them in
Fulton Market

How a once-
gritty meatpacking
neighbourhood has
become the location
of choice for glitzy
restaurants, hotels,
art galleries and even
corporate HQs.

*by Ari Bendersky,
writer*

Back in 2003 – having lived in San Francisco through the halcyon days before the dot-com bubble burst – my now-husband and I moved back to my hometown, Chicago. I hit my contacts to get work using my journalism and marketing backgrounds and, to supplement my freelance gigs, landed a job at a restaurant in the then-burgeoning but still gritty West Loop.

This restaurant, Vivo, opened in 1991 in a neighbourhood long populated with meatpackers, wholesale fishmongers and the like. The area had a seediness to it. When I told my mom where I'd be waiting tables, she said, "You're working where? Oh honey, that place is just hookers and tumbleweeds."

Streetwalkers aside, the intimate Vivo – a modern version of the classic red-sauce Italian joints that dotted Little Italy about a mile south – was a vibrant restaurant carved out of an exposed-brick interior. It featured a wall lined with empty wine bottles, fabric-covered wrought-iron chairs and the city's most sought-after table, up a winding staircase and behind a heavy velvet curtain. In the course of its 25-year life it pioneered what has become Chicago's hottest dining destination: Randolph Street.

It was here I'd come to work dinner shifts four nights a week, often leaving with $300-plus in my pocket after waiting on years-long regulars and tourists sent over by supportive hotel concierges. I'd open $150 bottles of brunello di montalcino while my guests indulged in truffle gnocchi, fall-off-the-bone ossobuco and whole branzino deboned tableside. Every day, as I'd circle for a parking space, I'd dodge aggressive meatpacking workers transporting boxes or pallets on forklifts along the side streets or on busy Fulton Market. The CTA's Green Line train would rattle overhead and blue-collar workers would grab a sandwich at JP Graziano's sandwich shop or pick up bags of fresh produce from the wholesale markets.

This was a working neighbourhood and an extension of the infamous stockyards that put Chicago on the map as "hog butcher to the world". The streets were full of potholes that would gather unidentifiable greenish liquid leaking out from the meatpacking factories. Maverick nightlife impresarios set up sprawling clubs inside warehouses and artists took over inexpensive lofts to create their masterpieces. More restaurants followed – Marché, Blackbird, Avec – until a new wave, started by *Top Chef* winner Stephanie Izard's Girl & The Goat, started flooding Randolph Street and, eventually, Fulton Market.

Here, chef Paul Kahan and his One Off Hospitality partners took a chance with The Publican, a German-style beer hall focusing on shellfish and pork. Then Michelin-starred chef Grant Achatz delighted global food fans when, in 2011, he opened his oft-changing Next restaurant and adjacent cocktail emporium the Aviary with its super-exclusive speakeasy, The Office. Soho House set up shop in a renovated 100-year-old leather tannery and belting factory in 2014. These openings, along with the installation of a neon Fulton Market District sign that spans the intersection of Fulton and Halsted streets, not only heralded a new dining destination but also the end of more than a century of meatpacking.

The owners of multi-generation meatpackers that had butchered countless cows, pigs and chickens for decades found themselves accepting multimillion-dollar offers from wealthy developers from as far afield as New York and China. Investors swarmed to buy block-long buildings, only to raze them and build hot new restaurants, hotels and company HQs for places such as Google and McDonald's. The meatpacking-owners may have laughed all the way to the bank but many of their workers were left without jobs.

Since Soho House opened, luxury shops have cropped up alongside high-end art galleries. The Ace brought its version of hip hotel culture to the area, and the Nobu and Hoxton hotels are next. Streets are being repaired. Ride-share cars seemingly outnumber the pedestrians they transport. A new CTA Green Line station opened in the midst of the activity. Anyone seeking steaks, chops and seafood – once butchered, packaged and transported out of the area – need only look to à la carte and tasting menus at restaurants such as Swift & Sons and Elske to secure their fix.

It's been more than a decade since I stopped working at Vivo and made a successful career out of writing. I stay in touch with some of my co-workers and we reminisce about our time at the restaurant that truly broke down barriers by opening in an area that, back then, made people scratch their heads.

Sadly, Vivo closed in 2016 after 25 years in business – it simply couldn't keep up with the influx of new players. It has left behind a legacy that turned a once gritty, working-class enclave into a glittery beacon of high-end dining and sophistication.

I must admit though, that just once in a while it would be nice to see a tumbleweed roll past a prostitute. But, unfortunately, those days are gone. — (M)

ABOUT THE WRITER: Ari Bendersky is a writer specialising in food, drink and travel. He has written for *The New York Times*, *WSJ* magazine, *Men's Journal*, *Wine Enthusiast*, *Departures* and more.

ESSAY 06
Field of dreams
Wrigley Field

———

Much more than just a baseball ground, the home of the Chicago Cubs is an integral part of the city's identity.

by Andrew Mueller, Monocle

Even if you've no interest in baseball, there's a good chance you've heard of Wrigley Field, thanks to 1980s cinema. The home ground of the Chicago Cubs plays a cameo role in two of the greatest Chicago films. Its street address – 1060 West Addison – is the misdirection given to hapless police by Elwood Blues early in *The Blues Brothers*. It's also one of the destinations visited during *Ferris Bueller's Day Off* (in the film, the game Ferris and friends see is the Cubs against the Atlanta Braves in June 1985, although the exteriors at Wrigley Field were actually shot during a match against the Montreal Expos later that year).

Built in 1914, it's the second-oldest still-functioning Major League Baseball ground, predated only by Fenway Park, the home of the Boston Red Sox. It's beautiful to look at – quirky and charming in exactly the way that more utilitarian modern ballparks are not. It retains its manual scoreboard, which has loomed over the field since the 1930s, and ivy of a similar vintage covers the outfield walls, a feature to which

baseball's laws have had to adjust: if a ball gets smacked into the ivy and lost, it's judged a ground-rule double. Not for nothing is Wrigley Field known as "the friendly confines", and on any game day it will be abundantly populated by people happy to explain this unique rule and other facets of baseball in merciless detail.

While many US sports venues have been relocated to featureless precincts on the city outskirts, Wrigley Field obstinately remains part of a neighbourhood. It's wedged so tightly into the residential streets of the suburb of Lakeview that the ground – and the games – can be seen from the roof terraces of adjacent houses (many of these have been converted into luxury seating and can be booked online).

But the physical properties of Wrigley Field, delightful though they may be, are not the best reason for a visit. Like any truly great sports venue, Wrigley Field has become vastly more than a mere arena in which athletes perform. It's a crucible for the city's history, a repository of its hopes and the setting of dramas crucial to local mythology. Its very name represents an understanding of that importance. Other sports venues routinely sell naming rights to whichever sponsor is willing to put up the cash, leading to no end of indignities – the Cubs' rivals from Chicago's South Side, the White Sox, currently play at Guaranteed Rate Field, in honour of some mortgage company. Wrigley Field retains, despite offers, the name of chewing gum tycoon William Wrigley Jr, who bought the Cubs in the 1920s and whose family retained control until 1981.

As befits one of the great sports grounds in the US, Wrigley Field has been the backdrop to one of the nation's great sporting stories – the heartbreaking, belief-beggaring saga of the Cubs, a team

> *"Wrigley Field has become a crucible for the city's history, a repository of its hopes and the setting of dramas crucial to local mythology"*

that became legendary at various points, either for being just plain terrible or for plucking defeat from the jaws of victory.

For decades, the Cubs were plagued by what became known as the "Curse of the Billy Goat". This bizarre hex dates back to a moment in 1945, when local innkeeper William Sianis was ejected from the grounds because fans objected to the stench of his pet goat, Murphy. Sianis muttered a curse as he was ushered towards the exit (his family further insisted that he sent a telegram to the Cubs' then-owner, Philip K Wrigley, declaring "You are never going to win the World Series again because you insulted my goat"). The Cubs lost that year's World Series to the Detroit Tigers and didn't reach another title-decider until 2016, when the curse was finally lifted with a World Series victory over the Cleveland Indians.

The eternity in between was punctuated by picturesque mishaps, perhaps none more memorable than an incident in 2003 that made one seat in Wrigley Field's bleachers (Aisle 4, Row 8, Seat 113) a Chicago landmark in its own right. This was the perch occupied by a Cubs fan called Steve Bartman during Game 6 of the 2003 National League Championship Series – the precursor to the World Series. The Cubs were hosting the Florida Marlins, and, at

one pivotal juncture, Bartman reached – as baseball fans do – to catch a foul ball that had been hit in his direction. In so doing, he spoiled the attempt of Cubs outfielder Moises Alou to catch the ball. The moment turned the game, and the series, and a mortified and terrified Bartman retreated into penitent hermitude, declining all offers – some potentially profitable – to discuss the incident. (Sportingly, after their redemptive 2016 triumph, the Cubs presented Bartman with a commemorative diamond-studded World Series ring, like the one awarded to victorious players.)

Wrigley Field does have considerable winter sport heritage as well: it was the home ground of much-loved local NFL team the Chicago Bears for several decades, before they moved to Soldier Field in 1971. But for more than a century, Wrigley Field has been synonymous with the US's consuming summer passion – and with Chicago. — (M)

ABOUT THE WRITER: Andrew Mueller is a contributing editor at MONOCLE. He has been to Wrigley Field once, in 2011, when he saw the Cubs beat the White Sox, 3-1.

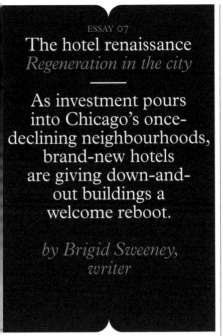

ESSAY 07

The hotel renaissance
Regeneration in the city

As investment pours into Chicago's once-declining neighbourhoods, brand-new hotels are giving down-and-out buildings a welcome reboot.

by Brigid Sweeney, writer

Every neighbourhood in Chicago has a tale of gentrification, good or bad. From the 1960s, when the city's original urban-rehabbers began transforming Lincoln Park into a pocket of affluence, to today, as trendy new restaurants and long-time working-class Mexican residents coexist uneasily in Pilsen, Chicago's story is one of renewal. And nowhere is this more apparent than in the city's hospitality scene.

One of the most successful examples of recent renewal is happening inside long-abandoned buildings in the Loop and other affluent North Side neighbourhoods. Rather than tearing these old gems down, investors are doing them up with both panache and a healthy dose of architectural and historical respect, creating boutique hotels with style to spare.

No recent hotel renaissance is more notable than that of the Chicago Athletic Association, a Venetian gothic beauty in the Loop. Originally completed in 1893, the building for years allowed wealthy Chicagoans such as Marshall Field (of department store fame) and William Wrigley Jr (the chewing gum magnate) to exercise, dine and sleep in plush surroundings. But after the club shuttered in 2007, a developer planned to tear down two-thirds of the building and erect a high-rise.

In 2012, to the relief of many preservationists, a group of investors including John Pritzker – son of the Hyatt Hotels founder – bought the building and has since poured a small fortune, estimated to be worth $100m, into a jaw-dropping restoration. Today, Loop office-workers and tourists coming from Millennium Park gather to enjoy the regal lobby, replete with three working fireplaces; the Game Room, filled with bocce and shuffleboard games; the Cherry Circle Room, an intimate bar with wood panelling and throwback cocktails; and the rooftop restaurant Cindy's, which offers majestic views of Millennium Park and the city skyline.

Shortly after the Athletic Association reopened its doors in 2015, another nearby architectural standout, the neoclassical former London Guarantee & Accident Building at the corner of Michigan Avenue and Wacker Drive, along the Chicago River, reopened as the

452-room LondonHouse Hotel after a multimillion-dollar makeover.

More recently still, the developer behind LondonHouse spent a small fortune renovating a long-vacant and dilapidated building at 168 North Michigan, built in 1912 by the famed architect Benjamin Marshall, into the sleek Hotel Julian. And let's not forget the old Carbide & Carbon Building, a nearby 1929 art deco landmark that was turned first into a Hard Rock Hotel and now has been reinvented once again as the St Jane, an elegant boutique hotel named after Jane Addams, Chicago's famed 19th-century social reformer.

"As well as attractive decor, historic details and culinary delights, these new hotels present an optimistic view of what urban evolution might look like"

All told, four painstakingly renovated, visually striking and architecturally significant hotels – which also offer vibrant social spaces, coffee shops and restaurants – have opened their doors within a four-block stretch of Michigan Avenue in fewer than four years.

A couple of miles further north, the rehab mania has continued at the new Viceroy Hotel, opened in a 1920s terracotta building that was the former home of the Cedar Hotel, a stop-in in the heart of the Gold Coast. The beautifully restored façade is matched by the hotel's chic restaurant, Somerset. Run by Boka Restaurant Group (BRG), one of Chicago's most prominent restaurant companies, it somehow pulls off a modern country-club vibe without seeming twee.

BRG is also affiliated with the Hotel Lincoln, another historic building across the street from Lincoln Park that has been revived after falling on hard times. Built in 1928, the hotel once hosted luminaries such as playwright David Mamet before becoming a Days Inn and eventually falling vacant. Hotel Lincoln reopened in 2012 complete with a scenic rooftop bar called the J Parker, gourmet coffee shop Elaine's Coffee Call and, more recently, the farm-to-table restaurant The Kennison.

As well as attractive decor, historical details and culinary delights, these new hotels present an optimistic view of what urban evolution might look like in other neighbourhoods. Standing in the Chicago Athletic Association's remarkable vintage ballroom, where stained-glass caps the windows and the ceiling still has the original ornate plaster "stalactites" tipped with light bulbs, it's easy to forget you're only eight floors above a Shake Shack. Yet they coexist. Perhaps, with more investment of this calibre and a commitment to respecting the unique past of each Chicago neighbourhood, we can look to a vibrant future. — (M)

ABOUT THE WRITER: Chicago-born writer, editor and staffer at *Crain's Chicago Business*, Brigid Sweeney has spent most of her career writing about her hometown – much of it from inside rehabbed Loop hotels.

ESSAY 08
Taller stories
Tribune Tower

Conceived as a monument to the city's favourite daily newspaper, the Tribune Tower is a soaring statement on Chicago's skyline.

by Tomos Lewis, Monocle

Towers, it might seem obvious to say, are meant to tower. To rise, to soar, to draw the eye skywards. Towers are aspirational. From the outside, at ground level, they make us feel small. From the inside, at the top, they make us feel like kings.

It's in this vein that, in 1922, the *Chicago Tribune* launched a competition for a new downtown headquarters to mark the newspaper's 75th birthday. The completed tower – according to the most influential of the *Tribune*'s publishers at the time, Colonel Robert McCormick – should be "the most beautiful building in the world".

Beauty, in this sense too, meant height: the new Tribune Tower should be at the forefront of the burgeoning architectural practice of building upwards. This was something that Chicago, like New York, was increasingly using as a hallmark of its built form, fashioning structures to echo its economic, cultural and political ascendancy.

That ambition came at a time when the word "skyscraper" – repurposed from a nautical term that denoted the mast or sail

of a tall ship – was cementing itself in the lexicon of architecture for buildings that soared. And the prize money ($100,000) reflected the prestige of the commission.

"The *Tribune* wanted to make a statement," says Jonathan Solomon, director of architecture, interior architecture and designed objects at the School of the Art Institute of Chicago. "In order to do that, it publicised the competition worldwide and that's where the architectural imagination of the building came from."

Some 260 entries were submitted from 23 countries, spanning the gamut of the increasing architectural philosophies of the time. The designs included Eliel Saarinen's second-placed entry – a stepped, church-like tower that would itself become an influential blueprint for several skyscrapers built in Chicago in the years following the competition. Then there was Austrian architect Adolf Loos's fanciful design of an oversized Doric column – designed to reflect the newspaper columns published daily by the *Tribune* and, arguably, the pillars that sustained the principles of journalism more broadly. That design, too, would become highly influential among postmodern architects.

"The new Tribune Tower should be at the forefront of the burgeoning architectural practice of building upwards"

"Its design is unique," says Solomon of the winning entry by Raymond Hood and John Mead Howells (the former would later go on to design Rockefeller Plaza in New York). Located on Michigan Avenue, across the street from the Wrigley Building and near Chicago's original settlement, the area plays an important role in the city's history. "It remains a site of experimentation and imagination and it's about the future of the tower as a form."

The architects conceived a neo-gothic tower, a cathedral of sorts to both journalism and commerce, inspired by the Tour de Beurre of Rouen Cathedral in Normandy, which was completed in 1507. Critics, however, decried the tower's gothic references when the design was unveiled, declaring that the winning building looked back architecturally, rather than to Chicago's future.

But the tower aimed to assert Chicago's ascendant status as a world city in quirkier, and perhaps more controversial, ways. During its construction, the *Tribune*'s foreign correspondents were tasked with retrieving fragments of some of the world's great landmarks, which would later be studded into the outer walls at street level. There are 149 "rocks" pocked into the tower, including fragments of the Taj Mahal and the Great Wall of China, a piece of the dome of St Peter's Basilica in Vatican City, a gargoyle from Notre Dame Cathedral in Paris and even a piece of The White House. A steel fragment from the collapsed World Trade Center towers in New York was added after September 11, 2001.

When the completed building opened its doors in 1925, nearly 20,000 Chicagoans showed up to see their city's latest architectural marvel. "Judges and society matrons, folks from out of town, a mother with a couple of perspiring children dragging at her arms, a sister in her heavy black robes, an old fellow who boasted he'd read the *Tribune* for 35 years, all these and many more packed themselves into the lobby of the tower and swarmed over every one of its 34 floors," reported the *Tribune*.

While the Tribune Tower spoke, through architecture, of Chicago's ambitions as a city – its hopes and sense of self – Chicago's urban landscape now evokes a different kind of character and urban aspiration. It's on the ground, rather than in the sky, that much of the city's most novel architectural work is underway, in several public projects from the Stony Island Arts Bank by Theaster Gates to the Chicago Riverwalk by RBA.

"Skyscrapers have always been the landmarks of capitalism," says Solomon. "They are the architectural type of capitalism and they come to mean different things over time. The Tribune Tower was built for a journalism corporation and we can, I suppose, lament the state or value of journalism today." (The *Chicago Tribune* sold the tower in 2016 and the building is being repurposed as a hotel.)

This shift in focus from architectural demonstrations of power in the sky to architecture for city-dwellers on the ground says something about how Chicago itself is moving into a different phase. "The quality of parks, the public role they play and the willingness of the city to embrace and invest in that has become incredibly important," says Solomon. "Capturing the value of that is really exciting and will have repercussions around the globe." — (M)

ABOUT THE WRITER: Tomos Lewis is MONOCLE's bureau chief in Toronto. His favourite stone in the walls of the Tribune Tower is from his native Wales: a fragment of Beaumaris Castle, built between 1295 and 1330.

ESSAY 09
Love/poetry
Chicago's poetry scene

The creative writing community in Chicago is sprawling – and in some cases the fertile ground from which romance can blossom.

by Jacob Victorine, poet

Arriving in Chicago in 2011 was surreal. With its parallel forms of the New York institutions I'd grown up with – CTA for MTA, Food & Liquor for bodega, deep dish for New York-style pizza – the city was similar enough to my hometown to make for an easy transition but different enough for me to feel off-kilter.

Up until then, I'd lived the entire 25 years of my life in New York – the last four of which I'd spent immersed in the Tri-State area's slam and performance-poetry communities. I'd competed at the Nuyorican Poets Café, the Bowery Poetry Club, LouderArts, Loser Slam and Jersey City Slam, participated in two different writers' groups, and joined a performance collective that hosted a monthly open mic at the Senegalese restaurant Le Grand Dakar in Fort Greene, Brooklyn. I'd even hooped in a blacktop basketball league sponsored by Greenpoint-based bookshop Word, which required players to pass a five-question literary quiz before setting foot on court.

So while I knew moving to Chicago for the MFA Creative Writing-Poetry programme at Columbia College would be beneficial for my personal and poetic growth, it also represented the loss of what I knew as home; not just my birthplace but the communities that had taught me nearly everything I knew about poetry. I couldn't carry my house on my back like the hermit crabs my brother and I once caught in buckets by the Fair Harbor bay but home still has a way of travelling if you let it.

Seven years later, home is my wife, Sarah, who I met on my first night in Chicago at our MFA meet-and-greet. The event was held at a retrofitted bar in Uptown, the same neighbourhood where I spent my first seven Sundays at the Chicago version of The Nuyorican Poets Café known as the Green Mill. This jazz club is where I got to know poets Emily Rose Kahn-Sheahan and Marty McConnell during the Uptown Poetry Slam.

While Emily sagely advised me to stop shouting my poems at another long-running poetry slam, Mental Graffiti (which she hosted at the time), Marty invited me into her home for her monthly Vox Ferus writing workshop. Both events now take place in Logan Square, where Sarah and I live.

Down the street from our home is Uncharted Books, the independent bookshop where I've been invited to read with former Columbia instructor Kenyatta Rogers, among others. In spring 2018, I stumbled into the local arts space Sector 2337, where Kenyatta was performing as part of a poetry crawl. Afterwards, I walked over to the next venue with him and Jennifer Karmin, who runs the monthly Red Rover reading series.

"Chicago's poetry communities have shown me that home exists in more than one place at more than one time"

Later that year, I saw Jen's co-curator, Laura Goldstein, read at my friend Sara Goodman's book launch at another Logan Square bookshop, City Lit Books. I'm almost certain Dolly Lemke was there too – she hosts the salon-style, semi-eponymously named The Dollhouse Reading Series.

In January 2012, Sarah and I attended the series to see poet Hannah Gamble read in Dolly's apartment – though we weren't there as a couple. Sarah showed up with the physical-therapy student she'd met on her flight home to Charleston, South Carolina, for Christmas. Jonathan could have been called "Beau" for his rugged, all-American, Kentucky-farm-boy looks, while I was more like Michael, pining over Marta in *Arrested Development*. Seeing someone else by her side

made me realise: "I've made a huge mistake."

In October 2012, Sarah and I saw Hannah perform again, this time at her book release hosted by the poetry collective West Side School for the Desperate. By then we'd been together for nine months. Nearly six years later, Hannah accompanied our former professor CM Burroughs to see us exchange vows in Sarah's church on Logan Boulevard, beneath a chuppah we'd built days before in our backyard.

Later, at the reception, Sarah and I read poems we'd written for each other, then toasted with our families and friends from all of our homes. Loved ones had flown in from New York and elsewhere; others were born-and-bred in Chicago.

While I will always call myself a New Yorker, the generosity of Chicago's poetry communities have shown me that home exists in more than one place at more than one time: people and memories stacked high as a hermit crab carrying all of its houses at once. — (M)

ABOUT THE WRITER: Jacob Victorine is a poet, fashion writer and multidisciplinary artist. His poems have appeared in journals such as *Columbia Poetry Review* and *Vinyl Poetry*. His first book, *Flammable Matter*, was published by Elixir Press in 2016. He lives in Chicago with his wife, Sarah, and their cats, Gilgamesh and Sita.

ESSAY IO

Gangster's paradise
Chicago on film

On-screen attempts to de-glamorise mobster crime have often ended up doing quite the opposite – and Chicago has long been the natural backdrop.

*by Ben Rylan,
Monocle*

Batman has played various roles in the 80 years since his comic-book debut: avenging killer, child's best friend, underworld vigilante, gothic knight. Whatever the interpretation, however, some traits remain unchanged. Batman is Bruce Wayne, a rich playboy who, despite living a life of limitless luxury, is drawn to the dangers of Gotham City after dark. Its corruption, urban decay and industry of glorified gangsters are the backdrop to countless adventures and an essential thread in a finely crafted myth.

Neal Adams, the artist behind some of Batman's most celebrated roles, cites Chicago's long association with underworld mobsters as the inspiration for Gotham City's rogue gallery of villains. It's a notion that Nathan Crowley, production designer of the three Batman films directed by Christopher Nolan, followed when he was scouting for locations. "At the end of *Batman Begins* we burnt down Wayne Manor," says Crowley, referring to how the destruction of the hero's home paved the way for the sequel's increased presence in the streets of Chicago. "*The Dark Knight* could be a city film. We thought, this city is the launchpad for whom Batman might become."

A city that spawns its own myths, for better or worse, had been weighing on the public consciousness in the years preceding Batman's debut in 1939. As the effects of the Great Depression lingered and Prohibition poured fuel onto an already flaming gang culture, Warner Bros released a film in 1931 that would help define the studio's brand of gritty cinematic realism for decades. In *The Public Enemy*, James Cagney delivered a memorable performance as Tom Powers, a brutal, amoral gangster who bootlegs his way to a life of luxury.

With Americans gripped by economic anxiety and its effects on lawlessness, many pointed the finger at the excesses and moral void of Hollywood. The head of production at Warner Bros, Darryl F Zanuck, sought to appease them by arguing that this picture would sell the idea that improving one's environment and education could lead people away from a life of crime – and he had a point. The savage fate of Cagney's character hardly ranks as a case study for anyone contemplating a career in bootlegged beer. But, ironically, the same qualities that made the film a classic also obscured its lofty ambition.

The film may begin and end with its social cause quite literally spelled out. But as a bloodied James Cagney confronts his mortality while stumbling away from his would-be killers in the pouring rain, or a smouldering Jean Harlow declares her hopeless attraction to a man who takes and never gives, it's easy to understand how generations of viewers have been seduced by the film without considering its deeper meaning. What might have been a cautionary tale instead etched Cagney and Harlow into popular culture as Chicago's quintessential rebels of the 1930s. Wreckless, amoral and ultimately glamorous.

This was the same year that saw the US's most notorious mob boss Al Capone capture the world's attention when, after years of brutal crimes, he was finally sentenced for tax evasion at the Chicago Federal Building. The city's daily papers relished the public frenzy surrounding high-profile crime cases with enthusiasm. A series of columns in the *Chicago Tribune* by journalist Maurine Dallas Watkins reported on the trials of two women who had been accused of murder. The increasing attention being paid to female criminals who had waded into strife by way of outlawed booze and suspicious deaths had led some to conclude that, in Chicago, attractive women could literally get away with murder. In 1926, Watkins adapted her columns into a play, *Chicago*, a satire

of the feigned notoriety of the so-called celebrity criminal and the basis of the Broadway musical.

Crucial to the success of *The Public Enemy* was its timing: shortly after the advent of talking pictures in the late 1920s, when excitement over the possibilities of cinema was feverish, yet before the encroachment of strict censorship in the mid-1930s. Alongside *Little Caesar* (1931) and *Scarface* (1932), the film is an essential ingredient in the stiff drink we now call the gangster genre and it helped instil Chicago as the outlaw's natural habitat. As *The Public Enemy* states in its closing chapter: "The end of Tom Powers is the end of every hoodlum." But Chicago's gangster-land myth lives on. — (M)

ABOUT THE WRITER: Ben Rylan is a producer and presenter for Monocle 24 and reports on film and TV. He received his first Batman costume on his sixth birthday and hasn't stopped playing dress-up since.

Culture
—— All about the arts

Chicago is the place where gifted comedians come to train, where hit podcasts are dreamed up and where young artists kick off illustrious careers. While New York and Los Angeles often steal the limelight as the cultural hotspots of the US, the Windy City is just as exciting, doing more than its share to keep the country's cultural offering bubbling.

Its tight-knit art scene is headed by the world-class collection at the Art Institute of Chicago but if you look to the smaller galleries you'll find equally exciting works. The best new talent is spawned here and there's a wealth of Midwest and US art to discover.

You can't leave Chicago without seeing some improv – think of any big Hollywood comedian and it's probable they learned their trade at the likes of The Second City and The iO Theater – and for music fans there's a rich history of jazz, blues and house to explore. This is the home of Herbie Hancock, Muddy Waters and Frankie Knuckles, and the city has a host of venues where you can get your fix well into the early hours.

Museums and public galleries
Well hung

①
Museum of Contemporary Art, Streeterville
Mecca for modern art

This is one of the largest spaces dedicated to contemporary art in the world. Founded in 1967, it moved into this new location – between Water Tower Place and Lake Michigan – designed by German architect Josef Paul Kleihues in 1996.

It's famed for hosting Frida Kahlo's first US solo show and the first solo show ever by Jeff Koons. Alongside the collection of 2,500-plus pieces from 1945 is a stellar line-up of performance art and talks about contemporary works.
220 East Chicago Avenue, 60611
+1 312 280 2660
mcachicago.org

②

Art Institute of Chicago,
The Loop
Extensive and expanding

With its temple-like façade
and two bronze lions standing
guard, the entrance to the Art
Institute sets the tone for the
treasures within. The museum
and art school were founded
in 1879, eight years after the
Great Chicago Fire, and have
had various expansions since,
the most recent being the 2009
Modern Wing.

The collection has grown too,
from a series of plaster casts to
some 300,000 works, including
12th-century Buddhas, Aztec
coronation stones, surrealist
sculptures and 20th-century
stained glass. Don't miss
the moody street scenes of
Edward Hopper, Georges
Seurat's pointillist impression
of a Sunday afternoon on the
island of La Grande Jatte or
Grant Wood's Midwestern
masterpiece (*see page 77*).
111 South Michigan
Avenue, 60603
+1 312 443 3600
artic.edu

③
Stony Island Arts Bank,
South Shore
African-American archive

In 2015, artist Theaster
Gates turned this former
bank into one of the most
fascinating exhibition and
research spaces in the city.
It's a triumph in cultural
research and preservation
and one of the most interesting
arts spaces in town, with a
focus on African-American
cultural history.

Stony Island Arts Bank
features books, magazines
and mid-century furniture
from the Johnson Publishing
Company, which produced
two of the biggest African-
American magazines, *Ebony*
and *Jet*. There's also the vinyl
library of Frankie Knuckles,
with some 6,000 records
owned by the late godfather
of Chicago house music.
*6760 South Stony Island
Avenue, 60649
+1 312 857 5561
rebuild-foundation.org/site/stony-
island-arts-bank*

Dr. Margaret T.G. Burroughs

④
DuSable Museum of African American History, Hyde Park
Preserving black culture

In 1779, Jean Baptiste Point DuSable, a Haitian trader of African-French descent, arrived in what was to become Chicago. He's now credited as the first non-indigenous settler here and the city's founder.

The DuSable Museum promotes and preserves African-American culture, of which the city has an abundance, with permanent exhibitions about Chicago's first black mayor, Harold Washington, and the history of people of colour in the US armed forces.
740 East 56th Place, 60637
+1 773 947 0600
dusablemuseum.org

⑤
Swedish American Museum, Andersonville
Homage to immigrants

Andersonville had one of the most densely populated areas of Swedish immigrants in the US, after thousands emigrated here in the 19th and 20th centuries. The Swedish American Museum is small but jam-packed with pieces from the Swedes' arrival in Chicago, showing what life was like at the time. It's also home to revolving exhibitions of Swedish art and culture, as well as the Brunk Children's Museum of Immigration, which gives kids a chance to dress up and learn.
5211 North Clark Street, 60640
+1 773 728 8111
swedishamericanmuseum.org

Going public
—
There's plenty of art to take in while you're wandering around Chicago. Look out for famous statues downtown by Pablo Picasso, Joan Miró and Anish Kapoor, and head to Pilsen to discover countless colourful murals by talented street artists.

⑥ Chicago History Museum, Lincoln Park
Back in time

The Chicago History Museum was founded in 1856 but most of its collection was destroyed in the Great Chicago Fire. It was later re-established with thousands of pieces from the estate of confectioner and collector Charles F Gunther, including Abraham Lincoln's deathbed.

The collection now comprises more than 22 million artefacts, including a textile and costume archive vital to the documentation of the city's social history.
1601 North Clark Street, 60614
+1 312 642 4600
chicagohistory.org

⑦ Reva and David Logan Center for the Arts, Woodlawn
Up-and-coming talent

This is the home of creativity at the University of Chicago. While class is in session, explore contemporary-art exhibitions by emerging and established artists, including students themselves, at the Logan Center Gallery, as well as other work on display in white-cube rooms, corridors and the café.

There's inspiration aplenty here for any budding creative; head to the lower level for the chance to stumble upon Henri Matisse's "Jazz" prints, gifted to the university by the Logans' foundation, for example. The centre also hosts an eclectic programme of concerts, screenings, lectures and exhibition tours – check out the website for more information.
915 East 60th Street, 60637
+1 773 702 2787
arts.uchicago.edu/logancenter

Commercial galleries
Painterly purchases

① Kavi Gupta Gallery, West Loop
Chicago's art hub

With two locations a dozen blocks apart – one on West Washington Boulevard (*pictured*), the other on North Elizabeth Street – Kavi Gupta is one of Chicago's biggest commercial galleries, turning the West Loop into a hotspot for art and elevating the careers of artists such as Theaster Gates (*see page 93*).

Look out for artists who have been underrepresented due to gender, race, location or work that might be deemed too conceptual for the art market. The gallery represents the likes of Roger Brown and Firelei Báez, and has a publishing company and shop in its West Washington Boulevard home.
835 West Washington Boulevard, 60607
+1 312 432 0708
kavigupta.com

③
Carrie Secrist Gallery,
West Loop
Youth of today

A Chicago native, Carrie Secrist (*pictured*) has been working within the city's art scene since her twenties, after starting her career at the Whitney Museum in New York. She has now run her own gallery for more than 25 years in the West Loop, and it's a great spot to discover bright talent across many different disciplines.

Secrist has a great eye for up-and-coming talent and represents an impressive roster of contemporary artists at various stages in their careers, including Andrew Holmquist, Stephen Eichhorn, Liliana Porter and Anne Lindberg.
835 West Washington Boulevard, 60607
+1 312 491 0917
secristgallery.com

2
Richard Norton Gallery,
River North
Making an impression

Located on the sixth floor of the art deco Merchandise Mart (*see page 116*), Richard Norton's gallery has an emphasis on 20th-century impressionist and modern US art – especially that from Chicago and the Midwest.

In lieu of the white walls and high ceilings found in countless other commercial art galleries, this space has a homely feel, with plenty of paintings to peruse. The location used to belong to Norton's father and grandfather, who ran an antiques shop there when the Merchandise Mart opened in the 1930s; you can still see the original sign hanging in the back corner of the gallery.
612 Merchandise Mart, 60654
+1 312 644 8855
richardnortongallery.com

4
Monique Meloche Gallery,
West Town
Finger on the pulse

Monique Meloche has a knack for spotting talent before anyone else and has been the catalyst in many a mid-level artist's career, including Rashid Johnson and Amy Sherald (who painted Michelle Obama's portrait in 2018).

"I'm in this to make art history and I work hard to help my artists right from their very early stages," she says. "I want to give them opportunities, advice and support to get them collected both privately and publicly – ultimately with work in museums that is provocative and enjoyed for centuries to come." Find out who is going to be the next big thing at her gallery in West Town.
451 North Paulina Street, 60622
+1 312 243 2129
moniquemeloche.com

⑤

Rhona Hoffman Gallery, West Town
Platform for the socio-political

Rhona Hoffman has been a leading figure in Chicago's art scene for more than 40 years. She established her original gallery – Young Hoffman Gallery – with Donald Young in the mid-1970s. It's credited with being one of the first places to exhibit Cindy Sherman and Barbara Kruger, and was pivotal in representing conceptual and minimalist art at a time when it didn't have much of a platform in Chicago.

In the 1980s the two dealers parted ways and Hoffman opened her own gallery, which today shows socio-political art from around the world. Artists include Michael Rakowitz, Sol LeWitt and Jacob Hashimoto.
1711 West Chicago Avenue, 60622
+1 312 455 1990
rhoffmangallery.com

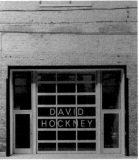

⑥

Richard Gray Gallery, Near West Side
Big names and beyond

The late Richard Gray trained as an architect to help with his father's construction company, only to end up founding one of Chicago's leading galleries. He opened his North Michigan Avenue space in 1963 as one of the first venues in the city where people could come and see exhibitions by the biggest names in mid-century art. The Gray Warehouse (*pictured*) followed in 2017.

The gallery now shows high-profile artists alongside others who have been long overlooked. At his two Chicago outposts (and a third in New York), you'll find work by the likes of David Hockney and Magdalena Abakanowicz.
2044 West Carroll Avenue, 60612
+1 312 642 8877
richardgraygallery.com

1709 West Chicago Avenue

Chicago is littered with tiny galleries, often run by artists themselves. This single building in West Town is home to some of the industry's favourite spaces.

01 Volume: Art meets design as owners Sam Vinz and Claire Warner display work with a focus on contemporary material and process-driven practices. Volume aims to question what US design means and to disseminate it to a global audience.
wvvolumes.com

02 Document: Aron Gent's cosy gallery celebrates the work of emerging Chicagoan and US artists, focusing on photography and digital media. It also doubles as a printmaking studio for local artists.
documentspace.com

03 Western Exhibitions: Scott Speh started his gallery as a roving exhibition space in 2002, before housing it here. Expect thoughtful pieces with narratives from a diverse and inclusive range of artists.
westernexhibitions.com

Comedy and improv
Funny business

(2)
The iO Theater, Goose Island
Training ground

Chicago's first-rate improv scene
is best represented at The iO
Theater. Opening in the mid-
1980s, it's become the place
for comedians to cut their
teeth, including Amy Poehler,
Tina Fey and Adam McKay.
"I like to think of Chicago
as a pure comedy town,"
says artistic director Kevin
Knickerbocker. "You can move
here, perform and experiment
with your comedic voice in
a supportive environment."
   The iO Theater nurtures
long-form improv so you may
see an entire play made up on
the spot, sometimes aided by
the audience. The side-splitting
Improvised Shakespeare Co
plays here every week.
*1501 North Kingsbury Street,
60642*
+1 312 929 2401
ioimprov.com

①
The Annoyance, Lakeview
Long-form laughs

Lakeview is fertile ground for
Chicago's comedy talent and
one of the leading theatres in
the area is The Annoyance.
Since its inception in 1987
it has hosted hundreds of
top comedians and plenty of
subversive shows. Like many
of its fellow Chicago venues,
it's a celebration of the city's
lengthy association with long-
form comedy.
   With all shows priced at
under $20, The Annoyance is
a prime spot to catch some of
the city's funniest, most radical
and most affordable talent. The
Super Human comedy troupe
performs here every Tuesday
and is a firm favourite among
the community.
851 West Belmont Avenue, 60657
+1 773 697 9693
theannoyance.com

The Second City

Chicago is home to the most famous comedy troupe in the world: The Second City. Founded as a cabaret in 1959 by actors, comedians and film-makers Bernie Sahlins, Paul Sills and Howard Alk, by the late 1960s it had played shows all around the world and welcomed the likes of Joan Rivers on stage, and in 1973 it opened an outpost in Toronto. In the 1970s, members included Bill Murray, John Belushi, Dan Aykroyd, Catherine O'Hara and John Candy – many of whom went on to feature on *Saturday Night Live* when it premiered in 1975.

The Second City has produced Emmy award-winning television shows and launched the careers of many great comedians and characters. It's where Mike Myers invented Wayne of *Wayne's World* fame and where Stephen Colbert, Amy Poehler, Steve Carell and many other famous faces started out. Its Chicago theatre also encompasses a training centre and the Harold Ramis Film School, the only film school dedicated to comedy.
secondcity.com

A chicken crossing the road? What next!

③
Laugh Factory, Lakeview
Manufacturing mirth

Doing exactly what it says on the tin, the Laugh Factory hosts some of the city's top stand-up shows. It was founded in Los Angeles in the late 1970s by Iranian-American comedian Jamie Masada, who wanted to run a stage where performers could earn a living.

Masada now runs clubs in five locations across the country, including this Chicago branch. Drop by to catch local stand-ups performing alongside famous names in the industry.
3175 North Broadway, 60657
+1 773 327 3175
laughfactory.com

①
The Empty Bottle, Ukrainian Village
Gigs and bites

This lively bar has been providing Chicagoans with the chance to see some of the city's best new bands since 1992. Today it's a firm favourite that attracts plenty of regulars: while it might be a bit grungy the line-up will appeal to any music fan, and there's plenty of dancing to be had on DJ nights, which continue into the early hours.

If you need a break from all the fancy footwork you can either shoot some pool or take advantage of the photo booth. Oh, and there's also an adjoining restaurant in the event that you require late-night refuelling.
1035 North Western Avenue, 60622
+1 773 276 3600
emptybottle.com

2

Green Mill, Uptown
All that jazz

This legendary bar has been *the* place to hear Chicago's jazz for more than a century – and it certainly has a colourful history. Famous for being a favourite hangout for Al Capone and other mobsters during Prohibition, it later played host to Frank Sinatra and Billie Holiday, and has featured in a number of films, including *High Fidelity*.

As well as its associations with gangs and jazz, the Green Mill is the birthplace of the poetry slam (*see page 87*). There's still live music every night and often the bar keeps its doors open until 04.00 or 05.00 in the morning, if you want to swing until dawn.
4802 North Broadway, 60640
+ 1 773 878 5552
greenmilljazz.com

④
The Riviera, Uptown
Legendary for live music

Built as a cinema in 1917,
before becoming a nightclub
in the 1980s, The Riviera
is now a beautifully grand
concert venue. The French
renaissance-style building
consistently hosts a top-notch
roster of performers, including
the likes of Red Hot Chili
Peppers, Robyn, Morrissey
and Kacey Musgraves.

It's worth checking out
what's on ahead of your
trip if you want to catch
some international acts while
you're in town – make sure
you book well in advance.
4746 North Racine Avenue, 60640
+1 773 275 6800
rivieratheatre.com

③
Thalia Hall, Pilsen
Landmark auditorium

At the heart of the Pilsen
neighbourhood since the late
1890s, Thalia Hall was founded
by John Dusek, who wanted a
space for bohemian arts in the
area. The building is modelled
on the Prague opera house
and sticks out on an otherwise
Mexican-influenced street. One
of the most ornate theatres of
its kind, it gained landmark
status in 1989.

Today you can catch great
bands and comedians, as well
as sample some excellent food
at the in-house restaurant,
Dusek's Board and Beer.
1807 South Allport Street, 60608
+1 312 526 3851
thaliahallchicago.com

Cinemas
Moving images

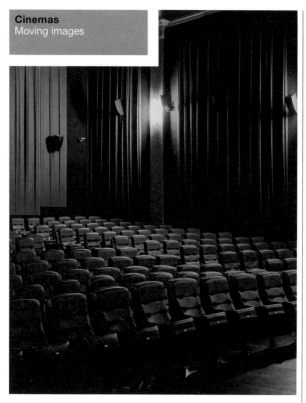

①

Davis Theater, Lincoln Square
Last man standing

There used to be five cinemas in Lincoln Square; now Davis Theater stands alone. The art deco building opened in 1918 and is the longest continually open cinema in Chicago.

Over the years it has been a German film house, a silent cinema and a place for puppeteers and other entertainers to perform. Today it's a classic neighbourhood cinema and a great spot to catch new releases in one of its old-fashioned auditoriums – and at a good price (adult tickets are about $12 each).
4614 North Lincoln Avenue, 60625
+1 773 769 3999
davistheater.com

②

Gene Siskel Film Center, The Loop
International programme

Named after one of Chicago's most respected film critics and writers, the Gene Siskel Film Center is a university-owned two-screen cinema in the city centre. Here you'll find a highbrow selection of films, with a particular focus on world cinema. It also hosts the largest EU film festival in North America every spring, as well as regular talks by film-makers on everything from animation to war flicks.
164 North State Street, 60601
+1 312 846 2800
siskelfilmcenter.org

Chicago on screen

01 **High Fidelity (2000):** This adaptation of the Nick Hornby novel transposed the story from London to Chicago. John Cusack plays the pretentious ageing muso, Rob, who runs a record shop in Wicker Park and is grappling with a failing love life.

02 **Ferris Bueller's Day Off (1986):** Supposedly John Hughes's love letter to Chicago. Matthew Broderick stars as Ferris Bueller, a slacker kid who skips school for a day of misadventures around the city. Look out for that iconic scene at the Art Institute of Chicago.

03 **My Best Friend's Wedding (1997):** Many a romantic comedy has been set in Chicago but this one, starring Julia Roberts and Dermot Mulroney, has stacks of swoonable scenes shot at some of the city's greatest locations, from the Lake Michigan shoreline to Union Station.

A little different

Run by the University of Chicago's film society, Max Palevsky Cinema specialises in documentary and independent films, usually by theme. It's the place to catch interesting flicks you're unlikely to find elsewhere.
docfilms.uchicago.edu/dev

Media round-up
For your eyes and ears

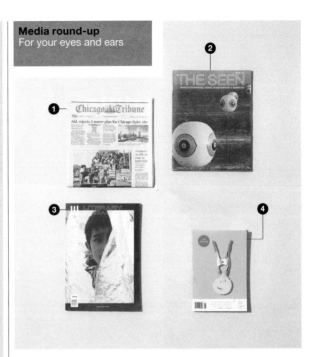

① Media
Page turners

When it comes to the city's newspapers, the **❶** *Chicago Tribune* is hard to beat. Since it was founded in 1847, this widely read daily has provided residents with both local and national news of the highest quality.

Culture vultures should pick up a copy of **❷** *The Seen*, a biannual journal of contemporary and modern art featuring everything from exhibition reviews to artist profiles. Meanwhile, literature buffs need look no further than **❸** *Make*, an annual print publication brimming with smart new writing and visual art. Finally, for personal, critical and journalistic essays, discussions on various topics, and reviews of just about everything, there's **❹** *The Point*.

Radio

01 **WBEZ (91.5FM):** One of the US's best public radio stations, WBEZ produces all sorts of exciting and creative audio. The birthplace of the much-lauded *This American Life*.

02 **Curious City:** Got a question about Chicago? Submit it to Curious City and they will attempt to answer it on their podcast dedicated to the area.

03 **Third Coast: 'Re:Sound':** Third Coast Festival is known as the "Sundance of radio" and when it isn't putting on its event it makes a podcast called 'Re:Sound', a celebration of brilliant audio craft from around the world.

Design and architecture
─── The only way is up

Restless, ambitious, muscular and mighty, there are few skylines as confident as Chicago's. After the Great Chicago Fire swept through in 1871 destroying huge swathes of the metropolis, the city became nothing short of an architectural laboratory, attracting maestros from Mies van der Rohe to Frank Lloyd Wright. Soaring land values meant that developers increasingly turned their gaze skywards and Chicago became the birthplace of the skyscraper – at 10 storeys high, the Home Insurance Building completed in 1885 created a whole new architectural typology.

But it's not all about lofty landmarks. From an angular mid-century prison in the heart of downtown to a brutalist spaceship-like church, surprises await around every corner. Chicago's flat topography is arranged in one of the world's more perfect urban grid systems, making it easy to explore on foot, but this glittering city is best viewed from the water: jump on one of the boats that ply up and down the river and prepare yourself for some serious neckache. Trust us, it's worth it.

Contemporary
New kids on the block

①

150 North Riverside, West Loop
In the balance

In a city centre tight on elbowroom, architects and developers have had to think outside the box – sometimes literally. Built on a skinny vacant lot sandwiched between train tracks and the river, and previously considered too tricky for construction, 150 North Riverside seemingly defies logic – and gravity.

A reverse of the conventional skyscraper model – which sees a wide, stable base narrowing towards the sky – this shimmering construction designed by Chicago-based firm Goettsch Partners rises from its slim footprint, tapering sharply outwards for the first eight of its 54 storeys like a pencil tracing the edge of the riverfront. Giant tanks hidden at the top of the building hold 160,000 gallons of water to help reduce sway during strong winds.

150 North Riverside Plaza, 60606
150northriverside.com

2

Millennium Park, The Loop
Park life

Until the late 1990s, this patch of prime real estate was little more than railway tracks and car parks. All that changed with mayor Richard M Daley, who, supposedly tired of looking over the unsightly plot from his dentist on Michigan Avenue, proposed a visionary new public space.

Today it's hard to imagine the city without Millennium Park. Highlights include the dynamic steel ribbons of Frank Gehry's Jay Pritzker Pavilion, the rambling garden designed by Dutch superstar Piet Oudolf and, of course, the signature attraction, Anish Kapoor's enduringly popular Cloud Gate (as The Bean is officially known). Join the swarms of selfie-takers drawn by its swooping reflective surface.

④

Spertus Institute, South Loop
Glass act

The multifaceted glass façade of this Jewish educational institute sits like a chiselled block of ice amid the historic buildings of Michigan Avenue. Constructed from 726 panes in 556 different shapes, it was designed by Chicago-based Krueck + Sexton Architects.

Driven by the Jewish principle of *bal tashchit* (do not destroy or waste), sustainability was a key concern: the windows are coated with a reflective frit pattern to control heat gain while a green roof retains rainwater and keeps the building cool come summer. Completed in 2007, the 10-storey structure houses exhibition spaces, a college, a 400-seat multi-use auditorium, a library and more.
610 South Michigan Avenue, 60605
spertus.edu

③
Poetry Foundation,
River North
Layer up

Established in 2003, the Poetry Foundation is an independent Chicago-based organisation that aims to promote poetry through public programming. It found a new home in this modernist-inspired structure designed by John Ronan Architects in 2011.

The two-storey building – unusually ground-hugging for this part of town – is wrapped in a perforated black-zinc wall that appears either opaque or translucent depending on how you approach it. Ronan envisaged the building as a series of layers that reveal themselves slowly, encouraging repeat visits.
61 West Superior Street, 60654
+1 312 787 7070
poetryfoundation.org

Tours de force

The Chicago Architecture Center runs an impressive programme of tours, all hosted by erudite volunteers: don't miss the 90-minute river cruise, which offers an unparalleled perspective on the city and its history. Its exhibition space is also worth a visit.
architecture.org

McCormick Tribune Campus Center, Douglas
On the right track

Rem Koolhaas's first building in the US is a rare contemporary island in the sea of Mies van der Rohe's mid-century Illinois Institute of Technology (IIT) campus (*see page 113*). Squeezed beneath the tracks of the elevated Green Line – which Koolhaas encased in a giant acoustic tube to muffle the sound of passing trains – the building acts as a student hub, effectively linking the two halves of the campus divided by the train line.
3201 South State Street, 60616
+1 312 567 3680
web.iit.edu

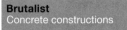
Brutalist
Concrete constructions

①
Metropolitan Correctional Center, The Loop
Prison break

This concrete correctional centre is a sharp triangular profile in the heart of the Loop – a prison within a prism, if you will. When its central location was announced there was a backlash from neighbouring banks and organisations but the Federal Bureau of Prisons stipulated that all new jails must enhance and protect the character of their urban surroundings. Harry Weese's design manages to do just that: three imposing façades perforated by narrow window slits resemble barcodes.
71 West Van Buren Street, 60605

②
Marina City, River North
On the up

Against Chicago's matrix of steel, glass and right angles, Bertrand Goldberg's twin Marina City blocks – giant, scallop-edged concrete cylinders – are like two fingers up to the rest of the city. When they were completed in the early 1960s, locals began referring to them as "the corncobs" but there's far more to the Marina City towers than their shape. Goldberg's "city within a city" was his solution for affordable inner-city housing at a time when professionals were moving to the suburbs.

The towers consist of a helter-skelter of car parks up to floor 19. Floors 21 to 60 are divided into pie slices of three different variations to create studios and one or two-bedroom units, each with their own balcony. There's also a supermarket, launderette, dry cleaner, gym and marina. Marina City offers all the attractions of life in the suburbs for almost 900 apartments in the middle of the city.
300 North State Street, 60654
marinacity.org

(3)
Seventeenth Church of Christ
Scientist, The Loop
In the round

Hovering like a travertine-clad
UFO among the skyscrapers
of the Loop, this Christian
Science church is a welcome
change of architectural pace
in this otherwise neck-craning
part of town. One of the
few standalone churches
in downtown – after being
destroyed in the Great Chicago
Fire, many relocated to more
residential parts of the city –
it has occupied this prime
piece of real estate since 1968.
   Harry Weese's brutalist
cauldron is largely windowless:
light enters the main
auditorium space (the design
of which is based on ancient
Greek amphitheatres) through
an oculus and skylight in the
centre of the roof, and the
Sunday school room in the
basement is lit by a hidden
sunken garden.
55 East Wacker Drive, 60601
+1 312 236 4671
christiansciencechicago.org

Skyscrapers
Height of success

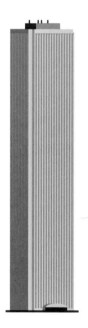

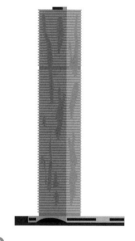

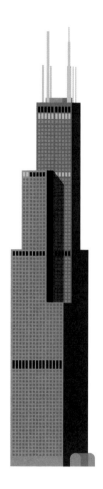

①
Aon Center, The Loop
Non-marble marvel

Completed in 1973, the Aon
Center – designed by Edward
Durell Stone and Perkins + Will
– once held the prestigious title
of the world's tallest marble-
clad structure. Unfortunately
the pernicious Chicago winters
had other ideas and the
43,000 Carrara slabs began to
buckle from exposure to the
city's temperature extremes.
The building was reclad with
granite in the early 1990s at an
estimated cost of $80m.
200 East Randolph Street, 60601

②
Aqua, The Loop
Running water

From a distance this 82-storey
mixed-use tower looks much
like the glass skyscrapers
that surround it – but get a
little closer and its sculptural
qualities become clear. Jeanne
Gang's dynamic design,
completed in 2009, employs
undulating concrete balconies
conceived to maximise views
and provide optimum shade:
the effect is of rivulets of water
cascading down the façade.
*225 North Columbus Drive,
60601*

③
Willis Tower, The Loop
Tall story

Previously called Sears Tower,
Chicago's tallest building has
dominated the city's skyline
since 1973. Accommodating
some 12,000 occupants across
110 floors, the steel structure
has more than 16,000 windows
and enough telephone cable to
stretch around the world almost
twice. Visitors to the Skydeck
observation level on the 103rd
floor can snatch views of
four states: Illinois, Indiana,
Wisconsin and Michigan.
233 South Wacker Drive, 60606

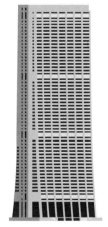

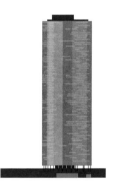

Chase Tower, The Loop
Far and wide

Conceived by Perkins + Will in 1969, Chase Tower swoops skyward from its central position in the heart of the Loop. Measuring 61 metres wide at its base, its elegant curved façades narrow to 29 metres at the top – a design that allows for more space on public floors near street level. The sunken plaza surrounding the tower has been home to Marc Chagall's mosaic "The Four Seasons" since 1974.
10 South Dearborn Street, 60603

 875 North Michigan Avenue, Streeterville
Pool up

Known as the John Hancock Center for almost five decades, this tapered tower in black aluminium and bronze glass now goes by its street address. The multipurpose building – built between 1965 and 1970 by Chicago-based architectural powerhouse Skidmore, Owings & Merrill – houses retail space, offices and private residences, plus the US's highest pool.
875 North Michigan Avenue, 60611

Lake Point Tower, Streeterville
Make a living

The only skyscraper on the east side of Lake Shore Drive, this residential tower was inspired by a 1920s design by Mies van der Rohe and completed by two of his former students. The original blueprints were based on a four-leaf-clover shape but these were rejected for the current Y-shaped plan to give residents greater privacy. It was the world's tallest residential building when it was finished in 1968.
505 North Lake Shore Drive, 60611

Mies van der Rohe
Master of modernism

①
Chicago Federal Center,
The Loop
Black beauty

Alexander Calder's dynamic
vermilion "Flamingo" sculpture
serves as the perfect companion
to this muted matt-black
complex. Completed in 1974,
five years after the architect's
death, the project consists of
three buildings – the 42-storey
John C Kluczynski Federal
Building, the 30-storey Everett
M Dirksen US Courthouse and
the single-storey pavilion-style
Post Office – organised around
an open plaza.

The whole site, which is
aligned on a rigid grid system,
is classic Mies: curtain-wall
structures conforming to
the key characteristics of the
International Style, namely
large panes of glass, flat roofs,
visible steel frames and no
applied ornament. In short, a
complete rejection of traditional
civic buildings fashioned
after heavily embellished
European architecture.
211 South Clark Street, 60604

In the house
———
Just under 100km west of the
city lies Farnsworth House,
a glass-and-steel box widely
regarded as one of the most
significant houses built in the
20th century. Painted white – as
opposed to Mies's usual black –
the single-room house appears
to float among the trees.
farnsworthhouse.org

*This is called
The Bean but do
not try to eat it*

③

330 North Wabash, River North
Final fling

Sitting like an austere black plinth between the fluted corn cobs of Marina City (*see page 108*) and the gleaming blue glass of Trump International Hotel and Tower, this was Mies's last building in the US, designed in 1973.

The boxy 52-storey building in steel and bronze-tinted glass, commissioned by computer company IBM, was truly envelope-pushing at the time. Due to the amount of software running through the tower, engineers had to pioneer a sophisticated temperature-control system that responded to Chicago's erratic weather conditions. The lower floors are now home to The Langham Chicago hotel (*see page 25*).
330 North Wabash Avenue, 60611
amaplaza.com

②

SR Crown Hall, Douglas
On campus

The building most often cited as Mies's finest work in the city – if not, the world – is no gleaming skyscraper in the heart of downtown but rather a low-lying pavilion housing the College of Architecture at the IIT. Mies served as head of the university's architecture department from 1938 to 1958 and during that time took it upon himself to redesign much of the campus: the SR Crown Hall opened its doors in 1956.

A pure rectangular form, the building is essentially a glass box hanging from four steel plate girders so as to appear almost floating. The open-plan interior is column-free and simply divided by free-standing oak partitions, truly embodying the architect's famous maxim "less is more".
3360 South State Street, 60616
+1 312 567 3260
arch.iit.edu

Early 20th century
Pieces of the puzzle

①

The Wrigley Building,
River North
Razzle dazzle

Rising like a dazzling white
smile at the end of the
Magnificent Mile, this elegant
structure commissioned by
chewing-gum magnate William
Wrigley Jr is arguably one
of Chicago's most famous
landmarks. Designed in the
Spanish colonial revival style
by Chicago firm Graham,
Anderson, Probst & White and
completed in 1924, it features
a grand clock tower modelled
on La Giralda – a minaret
that now forms part of the
cathedral in Seville.

The terracotta tiles that
clad the façade are actually
six subtly different shades of
white: ranging from blue-white
at the base to cream-coloured
at the top, this tonal shift gives
the impression of the building
getting brighter as it rises.
*400-410 North Michigan
Avenue, 60611
thewrigleybuilding.com*

③
Chicago Board of Trade
Building, The Loop
Grain ground

②
Tribune Tower, Streeterville
Hot off the press

In 1922, the *Chicago Tribune*
launched a competition for a
new headquarters to mark the
newspaper's 75th birthday (*see
page 85*). Beating proposals
from architectural heavyweights
such as Eliel Saarinen, Walter
Gropius and Adolf Loos, the
winning design by New York-
based Raymond Hood and
John Mead Howells was this
soaring neo-gothic construction
complete with gargoyles, flying
buttresses and an intricate crown
based on Rouen Cathedral.

On the day the building
officially opened in 1925,
nearly 20,000 Chicagoans
turned up to gawp at its quirks
and peculiarities. Embedded
in the outer walls at street level
you'll find fragments of some
of the world's great landmarks
retrieved by the paper's foreign
correspondents, and there
is even a network of secret
passageways leading to the
crown as per the instructions
of Colonel McCormick, the
publisher who commissioned
the building, in case it was
ever attacked.
*435 North Michigan Avenue,
60611*

This graceful skyscraper
designed by Holabird & Root
was completed in 1930 and
held the title of the tallest
building in Chicago for more
than 35 years. The structure
is topped by an art deco
aluminium statue of Ceres,
the Roman goddess of grain,
designed by John H Storrs.
The postmodern addition to
the south of the building was
built in 1982 and mirrors the
design of the original with its
symmetry and pyramidal roof.
*141 West Jackson Boulevard,
60604*
+1 312 435 7180
141wjackson.com

(5)
Carbide & Carbon Building,
The Loop
What a corker

Gleaming like a chilled
champagne bottle – or
perhaps, as some suggest less
poetically, a giant battery (the
Carbide & Carbon company
for whom it was built invented
the dry-cell battery) – this art
deco masterpiece is a vision
in emerald and gold.

Completed in 1929, the
design by the Burnham
Brothers features a polished
granite base and a main shaft
clad in dark-green and gold
terracotta, capped with a
15-metre-tall spire trimmed
with genuine 24-carat gold
leaf. After a stint as the Hard
Rock Hotel in the early 2000s,
the tower is now home to the
luxury St Jane Hotel.
*230 North Michigan Avenue,
60601*

(4)
Merchandise Mart,
River North
Think big

When this monolithic building –
so immense it once had its
own dedicated postcode – opened in
1930 it was the world's largest
building in terms of floor space,
filling two blocks. Developed
by Marshall Field & Co as a
central wholesale marketplace,
it was conceived as a kind of
city within a city.

Befitting its multi-purpose
function, the building's design
by Graham, Anderson, Probst
& White borrows elements
from warehouse, department
store and even skyscraper
constructions, imbued with
the art deco detailing and
geometric ornamentation
popular at the time. Today the
building remains the world's
biggest commercial property
and is visited by almost 10
million people every year.
*222 West Merchandise Mart
Plaza, 60654*
themart.com

Frank Lloyd Wright
Architect extraordinaire

❶
Unity Temple, Oak Park
Blank canvas

A few blocks from Wright's home and studio sits the sole surviving public building from his Prairie period – a huge house of worship commissioned by the local Unitarian congregation after their gothic-revival church burned down in 1905. They asked for a modern and affordable building: what they got was a bold and innovative design that broke with almost every convention of early 20th-century religious architecture.

The structure – sometimes cited as the world's first modern building – is constructed from exposed, reinforced concrete, appears almost impenetrable and has no steeple or spire. In fact, it features no religious ornamentation whatsoever – not even throughout the interior, which is flooded with warm light thanks to amber-tinted glass skylights. The congregation, by all accounts, were thrilled with the results.
875 Lake Street, 60301
+1 708 848 6225
unitytemple.org

②
The Rookery, The Loop
Modern update

When the ribbon was cut in
1888, the 11-storey Rookery
building was one of the most
prestigious addresses in the
city. Designed by Burnham
and Root, the muscular
structure with its rust-red
façade is organised around
a central court covered by
an elaborate skylight.

Wright was commissioned
to update and modernise
the lobbies and birdcage-like
court in 1905: he clad the
existing columns in marble
and added bronze chandeliers
with prismatic glass. Today
The Rookery is home to the
administrative offices of the
Frank Lloyd Wright Trust,
who offer guided tours.
209 South LaSalle Street, 60604
+1 312 553 6100
therookerybuilding.com

③
Frederick C Robie House,
University of Chicago
Prairie in its prime

Sitting in stark contrast to
the Victorian homes and neo-
gothic collegiate buildings
that surround it, Wright's
strikingly modern Frederick C
Robie House is architecturally
one of the most important
residential buildings in the
country. Low and elongated,
with dramatic overhanging
eaves and cantilevered roofs,
the house is the very distillation
of Wright's Prairie style. The
main living space is light-filled

and open-plan, divided only
by a monumental fireplace.

Strong horizontal lines
define the structure: even
Wright's trademark stained-
glass windows appear as
narrow ribbons dividing the
brick-and-limestone exterior.
Ever modest, Wright is said
to have declared his 1910
project as the "cornerstone
of modern architecture".
5757 South Woodlawn Avenue,
60637
+1 312 994 4000
flwright.org

④
Frank Lloyd Wright Home
and Studio, Oak Park
Work and play

Over the course of his career,
Wright designed more than
270 houses in the US; this
two-storey home, built in 1889
to accommodate the architect,
his wife Catherine and their
children, was the first over
which he had complete creative
control. Located in Oak Park,
the residence is defined by its
strong geometric forms and
dominated by a large triangular
gable. The highlight is arguably
the second-floor playroom with
its barrel-vaulted ceiling.

In 1898, Wright added a new
studio wing, which is connected
to the main house by a corridor.
It was here that he and his
associates drew up the plans for
some of his most iconic projects.
951 Chicago Avenue, 60302
+1 312 994 4000
flwright.org

Frank Lloyd Wright in Chicago

Frank Lloyd Wright arrived
in Chicago in 1887 at the
tender age of 20 and spent
the following two decades
living and working in the
area. While the rest of the city
seemed intent on growing
ever-skywards, Wright
developed his own distinctive
style of low-slung, ground-
hugging structures – often
characterised by their open
floor plans, overhanging eaves
and strong horizontal planes
– inspired by the vast, flat
expanses of the Midwest.
This would become known
as the Prairie style.

In 1893, after a number
of years working for the
prestigious practice Adler
& Sullivan (responsible for
many of Chicago's finest late
19th-century commercial
buildings), Frank Lloyd Wright
founded his own architectural
practice from his home in
Oak Park (*see left*). Today the
Windy City hosts the greatest
concentration of his projects
anywhere in the world.

1

Sullivan Center, The Loop
Talking shop

Situated on what has historically been described as the busiest corner in the world – the intersection between State and Madison streets in the heart of the Loop – this department store was designed by Louis Sullivan in 1899. It has seen various tenants in its time but Carson Pirie Scott & Co occupied the building for more than a century.

At street level, heavily ornamented cast-iron window frames seethe with motifs inspired by Midwestern prairie flora – an effective way to grab shoppers' attention.
9 East Madison Street, 60602

②
Chicago Water Tower, Streeterville
Liquid landmark

Oscar Wilde may have dismissed it as "a castellated monstrosity" but the Chicago Water Tower has a solid fan base among Chicagoans. Designed by William W Boyington, the gothic-revival tower is one of the only structures to survive the Great Chicago Fire – it was completed in 1869 just two years before the inferno – and is the second-oldest water tower in the US.

Featuring four identical façades crowded with crenellations, lancet windows, turrets and parapets, the building is essentially just a fancy encasement for a large water pump, intended to draw water from Lake Michigan. Today it hosts a small gallery run by the Chicago Office of Tourism and, if you're willing to listen to wagging tongues, a fair share of paranormal activity.
806 North Michigan Avenue, 60611

Monadnock Building,
The Loop
Electric feel

This brooding 16-storey office
building was the first in the
city to be wired for electricity.
Built in two parts between
1889 and 1893 (designed by
two separate firms), it features
a hefty, chocolate-coloured
brick façade that flares slightly
at the base to load-bearing
walls almost two metres thick.

Today the building houses
an assortment of small
offices – many belonging to
architects – and shops. An
ambitious renovation project
saw the interior restored to its
late 19th-century glory: the
glass partitions and gold-leaf
lettering are straight out of
a private detective film noir.
53 West Jackson Boulevard,
60604
+1 312 922 1890
monadnockbuilding.com

Visual identity
Look of the city

01   02

03

04   05

06

07

Urban details

01 – 05 Elevated train tracks: While most American cities replaced their elevated train systems with subways, Chicago has been running its L (short for "elevated") line continuously since 1892 – in fact, it's the only city in the US that still has operational elevated train tracks running through its downtown area. This web of riveted steel (and the associated thunder of a passing L train) has become a defining symbol of the city.

06 Chicago River: In an effort to prevent sewage from backing up into the city's water supply, the 251km-long Chicago River became one of the first rivers in the world to have its flow reversed in 1900 – no mean feat. It now runs away from Lake Michigan, through the heart of the city, to ultimately connect with the Mississippi. Every year the river – which effectively dissects the city – is dyed shamrock green to celebrate Saint Patrick's Day.

07 Movable bridges: Chicago's first movable bridge was built in 1834; today there are 52 within the city limits (43 of which are still in operation) – more than any other city in North America. Originally they were operated on demand but now they lift about 40 times a year between April and November. The majority are trunnion bascule bridges with counterweights that take roughly eight to 12 minutes to raise and lower.

Sport and fitness
── We can work it out

It should come as no surprise that many of Chicago's best options for staying active revolve around Lake Michigan. It's only natural that residents and visitors alike are drawn to activities such as kayaking and paddleboarding – this is a waterfront city, after all – and the epic views of the skyline make a river or lakeside workout just as uplifting for the mind as the body.

If the weather is against you – as is, sadly, often the case in winter – or you simply want to kick back instead of working up a sweat, there are also myriad indoor spas and wellness centres. Book yourself a snappy haircut or an indulgent treatment – or both – to ensure you're looking and feeling your best.

And don't forget, Chicago has an enviable sporting heritage. You can always get your competitive fix from afar by watching the legendary home teams in action. Hot dog, anyone?

Indoor activities
When the rain falls

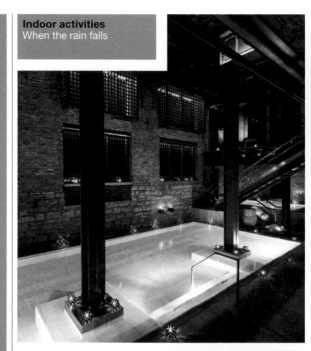

1
Aire Ancient Baths, River West
Bobbing along

You may think you can't float but a dip in Aire Ancient Baths' salt-water flotarium will soon prove you wrong. Book the Aire Experience to enjoy this and five more thermal baths (hot, warm, ice and cold plunges, plus jet pool), as well as an indoor/outdoor pool with a waterfall, a salt-exfoliation station and two steam rooms.

Exposed brick walls, wooden beams and the highest of ceilings abound in this one-time factory. The baths are lit from below, with flickering candles illuminating the paths between them. Sign up for a full-body massage or a Himalayan salt wrap, or simply waft from bath to bath until your finger pads are good and wrinkled.
800 West Superior Street, 60642
+1 312 945 7414
beaire.com

Do you
massage
beards?

❸
Chill, River North
Meditation and more

After 20 years in the finance sector, Laura Sage found herself yearning for a space to slow down and unwind. Such a place didn't exist in Chicago so she opened one herself.

Chill is a white-walled, minimalist studio offering yoga and meditation classes. Forget clouds of incense and gently chiming bells: the meditation here is modern, secular and accessible. There's also a massage programme with sessions starting at 20 minutes – perfect for a lunch break or between appointments.
222 West Kinzie Street, 60654
+1 312 222 1442
chillchicago.com

②
The Peninsula Spa, River North
Lap of luxury

The spa at The Peninsula (*see page 25*) specialises in Asian-inspired treatments such as the "bamboo massage", which stimulates energy through the use of traditional sticks, and the "Khushali Himalayan crystal salt scrub", which exfoliates the body with pink salts packed with minerals.

Make sure you arrive early enough to enjoy everything from the steam room to the relaxation lounge (complete with roaring fire come winter). The indoor pool on the 19th floor offers stunning views of downtown Chicago while the outdoor sun terrace is the best place to relax with a cup of herbal tea before or after a treatment.
108 East Superior Street, 60611
+1 312 573 6860
peninsula.com

Ⓐ

First Ascent Block 37,
The Loop
Sky's the limit

First Ascent has locations
throughout Chicago, including
the Loop (*pictured*), with
climbing walls to suit everyone
from children and beginners
to professionals. Sign up for a
class, buy a day pass or drop by
for a weekly session to connect
with fellow climbers. There's
a variety of challenges to keep
you interested, from standard
vertical walls to overhanging
climbs and walls that are
almost parallel to the floor.
    Locations are open daily
from morning until late at
night (exact hours vary by
day). If you need a break
from the walls, there's also a
gym that offers yoga classes
and exercise equipment such
as cardio, free weights and
climbing-specific training gear.
4F, 108 North State Street, 60602
+1 312 285 2337
firstascentclimbing.com

❶

Arsova Salon, River North
Pop of colour

The action at this downtown
salon takes place in a modern,
warehouse-style loft, under
the supervision of celebrity
hair stylist Anita Arsova. After
working on beauty editorials
and TV shows, she founded her
salon in 2013, bringing along
a team of stylists with whom
she had collaborated before.
    Arsova specialises in
colour, with an emphasis on
balayage treatments. Other
services include extensions,
styling and conditioning care.
500A, 747 North LaSalle Drive,
60654
+1 312 371 0773
arsova.com

Spectator sports

Sport is big in Chicago and the city's main teams have won world championships aplenty. Whether you're watching at the stadium or in a local bar, you're sure to be surrounded by hardcore fans.

01 Baseball: Choose between the Cubs, who play at Wrigley Field (*see page 81*) in Lakeview, and the White Sox, who play at Guaranteed Rate Field on the South Side. Tradition dictates you watch with beer, a hot dog and some popcorn.

02 Football: The Chicago Bears play American football at Soldier Field and fans arrive in hordes despite the often-frigid winter temperatures (many bring sleeping bags to keep warm). Before the game, you'll find many fans in nearby car parks (they call it "tailgating") grilling hot dogs and brats (sausages).

03 Ice hockey: Ice hockey is huge here because of the Chicago Blackhawks. The team have won the Stanley Cup six times since they were founded in 1926 and everyone has high hopes for them each year.

②
Blind Barber, West Loop
Cuts through to cocktails

Patrons reclining on the steel-and-leather chairs here may notice well-heeled revellers disappearing through an unmarked door behind the counter. What lies beyond is a dimly lit 1970s-style speakeasy with a rotating line-up of DJs, a dance floor, a cracking cocktail list and the gooiest grilled cheese in town.

The speakeasy concept may be common these days but Blind Barber doesn't rest on its laurels: the gleaming space out front is home to a talented team whose cuts are as sharp as their conversation.
948 West Fulton Market, 60607
+1 312 405 9929
blindbarber.com/pages/chicago

Date at the ice hockey. Wish me puck...

City beaches
On the waterfront

City beaches
Lay of the sand

Chicago has 26 beaches along Lake Michigan and each has its own distinct personality.

North Avenue Beach in Lincoln Park is one of the city's most popular stretches of sand, the place to see and be seen. Come for beautiful people, a cycle path, beach volleyball and tonnes of bars.

Oak Street Beach in Gold Coast is a hop, skip and a jump from a bunch of hotels and offers stellar views of the city. There's a massage tent, paddleboarding and an ice-cream van, so it's a good choice for lounging around or working out.

In Bronzeville, 31st Street Beach is family-friendly, with easy parking, a giant playground with sprinklers and calm water. Rainbow Beach in South Shore, meanwhile, is typically deserted, especially during the week. It offers bike rentals, is close to running and cycling trails, and even has a fitness centre.

Watersports
Splash out

①
Chicago Paddle Company, Kathy Osterman Beach and Ohio Street Beach
Paddle power

Chicagoans flock to Lake Michigan as soon as they feel a hint of warmth on their skin – and stand-up paddleboarding (SUP), which has roots in Hawaii, has gained a loyal following. It's a fun and low-impact form of exercise that's a cinch to learn and invites you to soak up the city from an entirely new perspective.

The Windy City may blow and bluster but, for the most part, the calm waters of the lake ensure smooth sailing. Sign up with Chicago Paddle Company for a private or group lesson, rent a board by the hour or find your inner balance with a SUP yoga class (just imagine your board is a rubbery mat).
Kathy Osterman Beach: 5800 North Lake Shore Drive, 60626
Ohio Street Beach: 600 North Lake Shore Drive, 60611
+1 312 970 0861
chicagopaddlecompany.com

Follow my lead!

②
Kayaking, The Loop
Own the river

At about $30 per person per hour, kayaking on the Chicago River is an enjoyable and relatively inexpensive way to work out while exploring the city and its architecture.

Several places offer kayaking rentals, tours and lessons, including Wateriders and Urban Kayaks. The former hosts architectural tours by kayak while the latter organises excursions all the way to the Monroe Harbor and back, plus sunset trips for the best night-time views in Chicago.
Wateriders: 500 North Kingsbury Street, 60654
+1 312 953 9287
wateriders.com
Urban Kayaks: Riverwalk or Monroe Harbor locations
+1 312 965 0035
urbankayaks.com

On your bike

Chicago routinely ranks as one of the top bike-friendly cities in the US. Find out why on these three routes.

01 **The Chicago Lakefront Trail:** This takes you through numerous neighbourhoods, including Lincoln Park and the South Loop with striking views of the skyline. Bear in mind it gets very windy in the colder months.

02 **The 606:** Chicago's answer to New York's High Line, this 4.3km-long elevated trail was completed in 2015. Once a freight line, it's now buzzing with cyclists, runners and anyone who wants to wander the Logan Square, Bucktown, Humboldt Park and Wicker Park areas.

03 **The North Shore Channel Trail:** Seasoned riders can try this 10.8km-long trail from Lincoln Square to Evanston, home of Northwestern University. It's paved along the river and gets a little crowded at peak times (10.00 to 14.00 on weekends) but you'll have it to yourself first thing.

Jog on

Chicago is home to many runners and most head to the lakefront to pound the pavement. It may be chilly come winter but the beautiful scenery – with views of Lake Michigan and the tower-studded skyline – will mean you almost forget about the brain freeze.

Walks
—— Take it in
your stride

It may be one of the US's
largest cities but Chicago
is also one of its most
walkable – at least within
each neighbourhood. Set
out in neat blocks on a
grid, it's easy to find your
way around and a wander
on foot is the best way to
take in the architecture,
shops and restaurants.

Here we take you on a
tour of four of our favourite
neighbourhoods, from the
art and Latino culture in
Pilsen to the warehouses
and industrial vibe of the
West Loop.

Wicker Park
Happening 'hood

Long labelled the city's most
up-and-coming suburb, it's
fair to say that Wicker Park
has well and truly arrived.
This vibrant neighbourhood
– once home to European
immigrants and those displaced
by the Great Chicago Fire
(before the inferno this was
little more than a prairie) –
is now packed to the rafters
with boutique shops, bars,
restaurants, farmers' markets
and coffee shops.

Much of the action is
centred around the busy
thoroughfare of North
Milwaukee Avenue, which
dissects the district on its
diagonal path to downtown.
Arrive armed with an empty
tote bag and an empty
stomach: Wicker Park will
obligingly help you fill both.

Wicker Park walk
Cafés and commerce

Jump off the Blue Line at
Western and take an immediate
right down North Milwaukee
Avenue until you reach
1 *Ipsento 606* on your left.
The second location from
local roaster Ipsento, this
handsome coffee shop, with
its exposed brick walls and
original tin ceiling, pours a
mean latte. Grab it to go and
wind your way through Park
No 567 up to **2** *The 606* (*see
page 129*). Running along an
old elevated railway line, this
4.3km-long park is named
after the first three digits of
the city's postcode.

Exit back onto North
Milwaukee Avenue and head
southeast towards the low-
slung red-barn-style building
on the corner of West Wabansia
Avenue. Welcome to **3** *Small
Cheval*, the little sister of the
famous burger joint Au Cheval

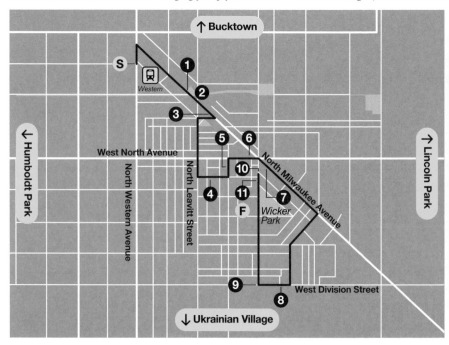

(*see page 34*). It may not hold quite the same prestige as its sibling but the burgers here are equally worth the trip (and the queues are invariably shorter).

Exit along West Wabansia Avenue and turn immediately left down North Leavitt Street, crossing West North Avenue and then taking a left down West Pierce Avenue. This street, like many in the neighbourhood, is lined with elaborate mansions built by Scandinavian and German immigrants at the end of the 19th century. The most impressive can be found at ④ *2137 West Pierce Avenue*. The gingerbread-style home was commissioned by Hermann Weinhardt to remind him of his native Germany.

For another interesting residence carry on down the street and turn left to reach ⑤ *1558 North Hoyne Avenue*. This mustard-coloured Queen Anne-style home became an American Legion Hall in the 1920s, hence the white cannon in the front garden.

At the end of the road turn right onto West North Avenue. On the opposite corner you'll spot the art deco spire of ⑥ *The Robey* (*see page 16*). The 89-room hotel is a destination in its own right, thanks to its ground-floor café and rooftop pool, which is open to the public from May to September.

Rejoin North Milwaukee Avenue and head southeast.

This entire stretch is lined with shops, bars and restaurants, some of which deserve your attention, others less so. Falling firmly into the former category is ⑦ *Myopic Books* and its three floors packed with about 70,000 secondhand titles.

Exit the bookshop and after a couple of blocks take a right down North Wolcott Avenue, continuing across the junction until you reach West Division Street. Here you'll find ⑧ *Penelope's*, a smart shop stocking mixed fashion and run by husband-and-wife team Joe Lauer and Jena Frey. The couple's new venture, Gemini (*see page 66*), opened across the alley in 2018. A little further down West Division Street on the same side is ⑨ *Velvet Goldmine* (*see page 59*), which is the neighbourhood's go-to retail destination for all things mid-century.

If all this shopping has you feeling hungry, head up North Damen Avenue, past the park that gives the neighbourhood its name, until you reach ⑩ *Dove's Luncheonette* (*see page 35*). Join the crowds that flock here for its Mexican food with a Southern twist.

When you're ready for a nightcap, simply roll across the road to the cocktail bar ⑪ *The Violet Hour*. There's no sign above the door so just look for the large mural splashed across the façade.

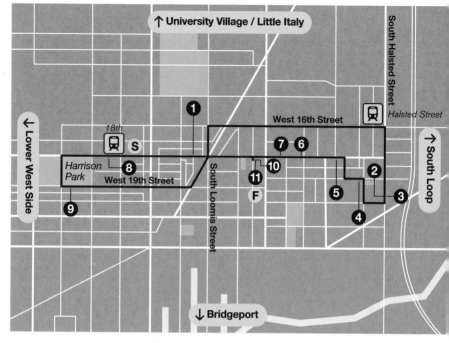

Pilsen
Artist magnet

Pilsen has been home to many immigrant groups, from Irish to Czech, but since the mid-20th century it has housed a mainly Mexican population. You'll spot tonnes of taquerias and hear mostly Spanish as you stroll around the neighbourhood.

It's also now home to an array of artists, who are giving it a new persona as an up-and-coming arts district. You'll find galleries all along South Halsted Street and urban art splashed across countless buildings; the neighbourhood is a hotspot for these murals so keep your eyes peeled.

Along with the artists have arrived new shops and restaurants – and the result is an area that blends fresh ideas with rich Mexican history.

Pilsen walk
Mosey through Mexico

Hop off the Pink Line of the L at 18th station, nip down the stairs and head east along West 18th Street until you reach **1** *Café Jumping Bean*, a neighbourhood favourite that has been frequented by Barack Obama, no less.

Grab a coffee then exit left and take a left onto South Loomis Street. Turn right on West 16th Street and stroll along the railway tracks admiring some of the street art for which Pilsen is famous. You'll notice it throughout the entire neighbourhood but this stretch is particularly eye-catching.

After a few blocks veer right onto South Halsted Street, where you'll discover an abundance of small galleries and artist-led spaces (some of which are by appointment only). Pop into **2** *Chicago Art*

Department, which cultivates and showcases brilliant new talent. The area, known as Chicago Arts District, hosts a monthly event called "2nd Fridays" when many of the galleries have their new openings. Head to the **3** *Information Centre* opposite to find out more.

Turn right onto West Cullerton Street then right again onto South Peoria Street. Veer left on West 19th Street, where you'll reach a giant warehouse called **4** *Open Books* – a non-profit literacy programme and an enormous treasure trove of secondhand books in the middle of a residential street. Here you can pick up all sorts of holiday reads starting at just a dollar.

After rifling through the shelves turn right onto South Sangamon Street and left onto West 18th Street. This is the main drag through Pilsen and home to the best shops.

Immediately on your left is ⑤ *Comercio Popular*, a shop run by local residents Miguel Cervantes, Marisol Carlos and Pablo Arancibia, who sell contemporary clothes and homeware made by Mexican designers. Further along on the right is ⑥ *Pilsen Community Books* (*see page 56*), a sleeker option if Open Books was a little too much for you. And a couple of doors down is ⑦ *The Shudio*; Pilsen boasts many vintage clothing shops but this one has the chicest selection on display, along with ethical and independent accessories and jewellery, plus lots of leafy plants.

After all that shopping you're bound to be hungry. Continue along West 18th Street, past the station where this walk began, and head to ⑧ *Carnitas Uruapan* for an authentic Mexican snack. This tiny restaurant has been operating since 1975 and its founder, "El Güero" Carbajal, is still often on hand.

There are always two queues so get in the to-go line, grab yourself a taco and continue along the street towards Harrison Park, where you can sit and eat before heading south through the park to the ⑨ *National Museum of Mexican Art*. Founded in 1982, it's said to be one of the largest Latino cultural institutions in the US, as well as the place where the two things Pilsen is famous

for meet: Mexican culture and art. There's a permanent display covering the history of Mexican identity in the US and, if you happen to be here in autumn, the nation's largest *Dia de Muertos* exhibition.

After perusing the art displays, exit left and head east along a residential stretch of West 19th Street, before turning left onto South Blue Island Avenue and right back onto West 18th Street.

It's dinnertime and we're eating at the Michelin-starred ⑩ *Dusek's Board and Beer*, located on the ground floor of the historic ⑪ *Thalia Hall* (*see page 101*), designed as an opera house in 1892. Enjoy some good food and craft beer before heading into the live-music venue to end your day with a performance.

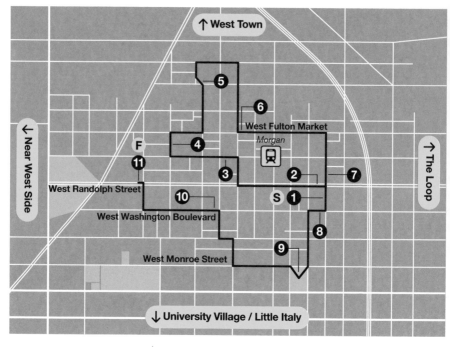

↑ West Town

↓ University Village / Little Italy

← Near West Side

→ The Loop

West Fulton Market

Morgan

F

West Randolph Street

West Washington Boulevard

West Monroe Street

West Loop
Industrial style

Sidling up to the river in
downtown Chicago, the
West Loop is the city's answer
to the Meatpacking District
in New York. Centred around
Fulton Market, established
in 1850 and recognised as a
district in 2015, it was once
the home of wholesaling
and meatpacking.

Although the area fell into
disrepair during the Great
Depression, it emerged in the
mid-2000s as one of the most
sought-after spots in the city
(Oprah Winfrey helped when
she set up the HQ of Harpo
Studios on West Washington
Boulevard in 1989, and
Google set up shop in 2015).
Today the former factories and
empty warehouses have been
converted into vibrant spaces
in which to live, work and play.

West Loop walk
In good taste

Kick off your walk with a
perfectly poured matcha latte
from industrial-style ❶ *Sawada
Coffee* (*see page 44*) – plus a
camouflage doughnut sourced
from the legendary Doughnut
Vault (*see page 44*) if you need
a sugar hit. Energised and
ready to go, exit left and at
the end of the block turn left
onto West Randolph Street
(turn right onto the same
road and you'll soon see
why it's commonly known
as "Restaurant Row").

After checking out the
latest offerings from men's
and womenswear shop
❷ *Billy Reid* (*see page 67*) –
the first of its kind to open in
the neighbourhood in 2015 in
a former distribution centre
for butchers' paper – cross
over West Randolph Street and
continue along it until you hit
North Aberdeen Street. Turn

right then veer left onto Lake
Street, hugging the overhead
tracks, and on your left you'll
find ❸ *Rider for Life* (*see page
61*), a treasure trove of clothes,
accessories and homeware.

Continue along Lake
Street then head right onto
North Elizabeth Street. Up
ahead is ❹ *Kavi Gupta Gallery*
(*see page 95*), a contemporary
art gallery which has a second
location on Washington
Boulevard. After you've had
your fill of art, keep walking
and turn right onto West Fulton
Market, then left when you
hit North Racine Avenue.
Cross over the railway tracks
(keep an ear out for the bell
signalling approaching trains)
and turn right into the car
park before you reach West
Hubbard Street.

Tucked away in a rather
nondescript building is the
headquarters of stationery
stalwart ❺ *Field Notes* (*see page
55*). Take a leaf through the

Address book

01 **Sawada Coffee**
    112 North Green
    Street, 60607
    +1 312 754 0431
    sawadacoffee.com
02 **Billy Reid**
    845 West Randolph
    Street, 60607
    +1 312 614 1503
    billyreid.com
03 **Rider for Life**
    1115 West Lake
    Street, 60607
    +1 312 243 0464
    riderforlife.myshopify.com
04 **Kavi Gupta Gallery**
    219 North Elizabeth
    Street, 60607
    +1 312 496 3552
    kavigupta.com
05 **Field Notes**
    401 North Racine
    Avenue, 60642
    +1 312 243 1107
    fieldnotesbrand.com
06 **Morlen Sinoway Atelier**
    1052 West Fulton
    Market, 60607
    +1 312 432 0100
    morlensinoway.com
07 **Little Goat Diner**
    820 West Randolph
    Street, 60607
    +1 312 888 3455
    littlegoatchicago.com
08 **Andrew Rafacz Gallery**
    835 West Washington
    Boulevard, 60607
    +1 312 404 9188
    andrewrafacz.com
09 **Mary Bartelme Park**
    115 South Sangamon
    Street, 60607
10 **The Press Room**
    1134 West Washington
    Boulevard, 60607
    +1 331 240 1914
    pressroomchicago.com
11 **Elske**
    1350 West Randolph
    Street, 60607
    +1 312 733 1314
    elskerestaurant.com

brand's latest notebooks while enjoying a sneak peek of its snappy Midwest offices.

Turn right onto West Hubbard Street then hang a right again onto North Aberdeen Street. Walk straight until you hit West Fulton Market. On the corner is homeware shop ❻ *Morlen Sinoway Atelier*, where you can pick up everything from jewellery and ceramics to custom-made rugs and bespoke furniture.

Exit left and continue along West Fulton Market until you reach North Green Street. Turn right then stop for a bite to eat at ❼ *Little Goat Diner*, a classic Chicago stop-in on the corner of West Randolph Street. Slide into a booth or hop up onto a swivelling bar stool and sink your teeth into something suitably diner-y – the Fat Elvis Waffles, perhaps, or the Big Biscuit and Gravy?

When your stomach is satisfied, continue on your way and, after crossing West Washington Boulevard, turn right. This wide stretch is big on galleries and the red-brick building ahead is home to a handful. ❽ *Andrew Rafacz Gallery* puts on fine exhibitions of both emerging and established artists.

Nip left onto North Peoria Street and keep walking until you reach ❾ *Mary Bartelme Park*, a leafy green space on the site of a former hospital. Visit

the viewing hill, zigzag up and down the diagonal paths, then leave through the northwest exit via the five stainless-steel gates of the fountain plaza.

Head west along West Monroe Street and turn right onto South Aberdeen Street. Next it's left onto West Madison Street, right onto North May Street and left onto West Washington Boulevard.

By now you'll most certainly be ready for a cocktail at the low-lit basement bar ❿ *The Press Room*. Try the Penicillin – tastier than it sounds, with scotch, honey, lemon and ginger – then, thirst quenched, continue along the same road until you reach North Ada Street. Turn right and, just across West Randolph Street, you'll spy ⓫ *Elske* (*see page 28*), bringing a touch of Scandi food and decor to the West Loop. Time for dinner.

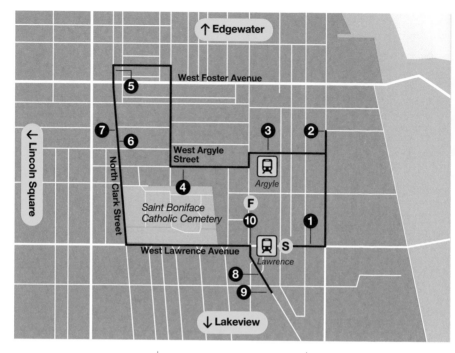

Uptown
On the rise

Uptown has a long and storied history stretching back to Chicago's notorious gangster era. Between the 1920s and 1940s the neighbourhood saw much activity at its upscale ballrooms, including the Aragon and Riviera, which brought in live bands for jazz and swing shows and today welcome big-name acts such as Robyn, Rüfüs Du Sol and Greta Van Fleet.

Aside from all the theatres, Uptown – an eclectic neighbourhood once again on the rise – has beautiful beaches, green parks and fantastic restaurants. It also has a vibrant Asian enclave featuring some of the best Vietnamese, Thai and Chinese spots in Chicago.

Uptown walk
From gay bars to gangster dives

Take the L to Lawrence and walk east to start your day at the uber-hip ❶ *Lawrence House*, an art deco apartment building dating back to the 1920s. Grab a coffee at the Heritage Outpost or a bite at 3 Squares Diner and then linger in the beautiful lobby to check out the once-hidden stained-glass ceiling and local photography. (Come back at night for a stronger drink at lively cocktail bar Larry's.)

Upon leaving, turn left and take another left at the traffic lights onto North Sheridan Road, walking a few blocks to ❷ *Tweet/Big Chicks*. During the day Tweet offers breakfast and lunch; enjoy a couple of its organic options or indulge in one of the breakfast burritos with a Bloody Mary spiked with spicy Sriracha. At night the space turns into the

welcoming Big Chicks gay bar, complete with legendary dance floor.

Pop back down to West Argyle Street and turn right. See the pagoda on top of the train tracks? You've now entered ❸ *Asia on Argyle*, where you can grab delicious pastries at La Patisserie P, pho at Tank Noodle, tableside Peking duck service at Sun Wah BBQ, banh mi at Ba Le or Thai street food at Immm Rice & Beyond.

Continue west and across North Broadway towards ❹ *Saint Augustine College*, which was the home of Essanay Studios. Here stars such as Charlie Chaplin and Gloria Swanson filmed some of the biggest silent films of the early 1900s.

Walk a half-block and veer right onto North Glenwood Avenue, heading towards the historic Lakewood-Balmoral neighbourhood. Marvel at the beautiful old homes then

turn left on West Farragut Avenue to walk towards North Clark Street, where you'll find ❺ *Scout*, a cherished urban antiques shop stocking treasures such as refurbished lamps, leather chairs and metal bookcases.

Exit left and stroll down North Clark Street through the former Swedish stronghold of Andersonville, now home to boutiques, cafés and restaurants. Cross West Foster Avenue back into Uptown and stock up on all your cookware needs at ❻ *The Wooden Spoon*, where you can also sign up for cooking classes. Next, walk across the street, step through the faux-launderette façade and enter the ❼ *Chicago Magic Lounge*, the city's premiere house of mind-blowing upfront magic, with three performance spaces.

Now it's time to sweat off all that snacking. Walk south along North Clark Street and

turn left onto West Lawrence Avenue. Continue for about 10 minutes, walking alongside Saint Boniface Catholic Cemetery, until you once again hit North Broadway, and turn right. You'll see the Riviera theatre (*see page 101*) in front of you and around the bend you'll find ❽ *First Ascent* bouldering gym, which welcomes beginners and seasoned climbers alike.

Dinner awaits at the intimate 20-seat ❾ *Brass Heart*, about half a block south on North Broadway. Michelin-starred chef Matt Kerney offers a seasonal tasting menu, including an out-of-this-world vegan option – which is perhaps surprising considering Kerney earned his star at the nose-to-tail, meat-heavy Longman & Eagle (*see page 39*).

After dinner exit left and stroll back along North Broadway to ❿ *Green Mill* (*see page 100*). This historic jazz dive dates back to the early 1900s and was a haunt of notorious gangster Al Capone. These days you can find nightly music, late-night jam sessions and, on Sundays, the famous Uptown Poetry Slam, which originated here. Stay late and stumble back to the Lawrence L station (or hop in a taxi) for whatever the night has in store for you next.

Address book

01 **Lawrence House**
   1020 West Lawrence Avenue, 60640
   +1 773 234 0321
   flatslife.com

02 **Tweet/Big Chicks**
   5020-5024 North Sheridan Road, 60640
   Tweet:
   +1 773 728 5576
   tweet.biz
   Big Chicks:
   +1 773 728 5511
   bigchicks.com

03 **Asia on Argyle**
   1118 West Argyle Street, 60640

04 **Saint Augustine College**
   1345 West Argyle Street, 60640
   +1 773 878 8756
   staugustine.edu

05 **Scout**
   5221 North Clark Street, 60640
   +1 773 275 5700
   scoutchicago.com

06 **The Wooden Spoon**
   5047 North Clark Street, 60640
   +1 773 293 3190
   woodenspoonchicago.com

07 **Chicago Magic Lounge**
   5050 North Clark Street, 60640
   +1 312 366 4500
   chicagomagiclounge.com

08 **First Ascent**
   4718 North Broadway, 60640
   +1 773 275 1212
   firstascentclimbing.com

09 **Brass Heart**
   4662 North Broadway, 60640
   +1 773 564 9680
   brassheartrestaurant.com

10 **Green Mill**
   4802 North Broadway, 60640
   +1 773 878 5552
   greenmilljazz.com

Resources
—— Inside knowledge

The third-largest city in the US, the birthplace of the skyscraper and home to the blues, Chicago has plenty to keep a traveller happily occupied. To help you make the most of your trip, however, we have compiled a list of insider tips and information, from reading recommendations and a playlist to what time of the year to go and how to get from the airport to the city. Plus, some local lingo to boot.

Transport
Getting around town

01 Flights: Whether you're arriving on a domestic or international flight, you'll most likely land at the sprawling O'Hare International, one of the 10 busiest airports in the world. The quickest, easiest and cheapest way into the city from here is via the Blue Line of the 24-hour L train; a one-way trip costs $5 (a shuttle bus connects Terminal 5 with the station, which is in Terminal 2). If you take a taxi, bear in mind that the traffic, and therefore the fare, varies wildly. If you arrive at the smaller Midway International, hop on the Orange Line of the L, which costs $2.25 and takes about 35 minutes, or hail a taxi (up to $30 for a 20-minute trip).

02 Train: If you're travelling to Chicago by Amtrak train, you'll arrive at Union Station in the Loop. The Chicago Transit Authority (CTA) runs both the subway and elevated trains (the L), as well as the city's buses. The L's eight colour-coded lines serve more than 140 stations. Buy a one-day ($10), three-day ($20) or seven-day ($28) Visitor Pass, which will work on both the train and the bus, or opt for a pay-as-you-go Transit Card.

03 Buses: You can either pay for the bus by cash ($2.25 per journey) or with one of the above cards. Most of the routes travel north-south or east-west.

04 Taxis: It's easy to hail a cab and fares start at $3.25. Ride-sharing apps are also reliable.

05 Bike: Chicago boasts plenty of cycle lanes and wide streets. The bike-sharing system, Divvy Bikes, has more than 580 docking stations across the city.

06 Walking: Chicago is a surprisingly big city: something that looks close on a map can be a trek. But once you're in the right neighbourhood, walking is your best bet.

City reading
Turning over a new leaf

01 Upton Sinclair, 'The Jungle' (1906): A portrayal of the poor working conditions of Chicago's meatpacking industry at the start of the 20th century.

02 Saul Bellow, 'The Adventures of Augie March' (1953): Bellow's third book follows the ups and downs of Augie March in Chicago during the Great Depression. Martin Amis called it "the Great American Novel".

03 Barack Obama, 'Dreams from My Father' (1995): The former president's candid memoir explores themes of race, identity and belonging through the events that took place in his early years in Chicago and Honolulu.

04 Audrey Niffenegger, 'The Time Traveler's Wife' (2003): This magical debut novel by Chicago-based Niffenegger portrays the relationship between art student Clare and librarian Henry.

05 Kathleen Rooney, 'O, Democracy!' (2014): A funny and sad exploration of US politics and the challenges of being a good citizen.

Best events
Dates for the diary

01 St Patrick's Day Parade, Columbus Drive: It's hard to ignore this particular parade. The celebrations begin with the dyeing of the Chicago River green at 09.00.
March,
chicagostpatricksday parade.org

02 Chicago Flower & Garden Show, Navy Pier: Founded in 1847, this flower show includes talks and workshops.
March,
chicagoflower.com

03 Chicago Blues Festival, Millennium Park: This three-day event is one of the biggest free blues festivals in the world. Past performers include the late Ray Charles.
June

04 Taste of Chicago, Grant Park: Sample your way through the stalls of this family-friendly food festival.
July

05 Chicago Jazz Festival, citywide: Four days devoted to jazz, both past and present, centred on downtown's Millennium Park.
August/September,
jazzinchicago.org/jazzfest

06 Expo Chicago, Navy Pier: The International Exposition of Contemporary & Modern Art opens the autumn art season each year.
September,
expochicago.com

07 Chicago International Film Festival: Established by film-maker Michael Kutza as an alternative to the usual flicks in cinemas.
October,
chicagofilmfestival.com

08 Bank of America Chicago Marathon, citywide: Runners from more than 100 countries fly into Chicago to race across the finish line in Grant Park.
October,
chicagomarathon.com

09 Magnificent Mile Lights Festival, Michigan Avenue: Kick off the Christmas season at this winter wonderland between Wacker Drive and Oak Street.
November,
themagnificentmile.com/ lights-festival

City in numbers
Facts and figures

01 1837: First recognised as a city
02 1885: First skyscraper built
03 2.7 million: Population
04 More than 200: Theatres
05 1915: The term "jazz" first used in Chicago
06 4.3km: Length of The 606
07 More than 320km: Bike lanes
08 87mph: Strongest wind (recorded in 1894)

Vocabulary
Local lingo

01 The Bean: Nickname for Anish Kapoor's "Cloud Gate"
02 Pop: Soda
03 The L: The elevated train
04 Washroom: Toilet
05 The Hawk: Cool breeze off Lake Michigan
06 Show: Not a film, not a movie, but a show
07 LSD: Lake Shore Drive
08 Gym shoes: Trainers
09 The Lake: Lake Michigan
10 Dip: Word for "leaving"

Soundtrack to the city
Top tunes

01 Robert Johnson, 'Sweet Home Chicago': Despite the confusing geographical references to both California and Chicago, this bluesy number – which has been covered by both Buddy Guy and Eric Clapton – has become something of an anthem for the Windy City.

02 Frank Sinatra, 'My Kind of Town (Chicago Is)': Composer Jimmy Van Heusen and lyricist Sammy Cahn wrote this homage to Chicago for the 1964 musical *Robin and the 7 Hoods*, starring Frank Sinatra – who went on to record many more versions of the song.

03 Duran Duran, 'Lake Shore Driving': A guitar-heavy instrumental tune, first performed in 1988, to blast from the speakers as you drive along Lake Michigan.

04 Sufjan Stevens, 'Chicago': This 2005 acoustic track from the US singer-songwriter's album *Illinois* tells the semi-autobiographical tale of an idealistic young man on a road trip to the city.

05 Kanye West, 'Homecoming': One to listen to as you land at O'Hare International. Featuring lyrics such as "fireworks at Lake Michigan" and, for reasons unknown, Coldplay's Chris Martin. "If you don't know by now, I'm talking 'bout Chi-Town!"

About Monocle
—— Step inside

London HQ
—
Our editorial
office is in
Marylebone

In 2007, Monocle was launched as a monthly magazine briefing on global affairs, business, culture, design and much more. We believed there was a globally minded audience of readers who were hungry for opportunities and experiences beyond their national borders.

Today Monocle is a complete media brand with print, audio and online elements – not to mention our expanding network of shops and cafés. Besides our London HQ we have international bureaux in Toronto, Tokyo, Los Angeles, Zürich and Hong Kong, with more on the way. We continue to grow and flourish and at our core is the simple belief that there will always be a place for a print brand that is committed to telling fresh stories and sending photographers on assignments. It's also a case of knowing that our success is all down to the readers, advertisers and collaborators who have supported us along the way.

1
International bureaux
Boots on the ground

We're based in London and have bureaux in Hong Kong, Tokyo, Zürich, Toronto and Los Angeles. We also call upon reports from our contributors in more than 35 cities around the world. For this guide, MONOCLE reporters Chloë Ashby, Joe Pickard and Holly Fisher decamped to Chicago to explore all that the Windy City has to offer. They also called on various contacts in the city to ensure that we have covered the best in food, culture, retail, hospitality and more.

2
Online
Digital delivery

We have a dynamic website: *monocle.com*. As well as being the place to hear our radio station, Monocle 24, the site presents our films, which are beautifully shot and edited by our in-house team and provide a fresh perspective on our stories. Check out the films celebrating the cities that make up our Travel Guide Series before you explore the rest of the site.

3
Retail and cafés
Food for thought

Via our shops in Hong Kong, Toronto, Zürich, Tokyo and London we sell products that cater to our readers' tastes and are produced in collaboration with brands we believe in. We also have cafés in Tokyo, Zürich and London. And if you are in the UK capital visit the Kioskafé in Paddington, which combines good coffee and great reads.

4

Print
Committed to the page

MONOCLE is published 10 times a year. We also produce two standalone publications – THE FORECAST, packed with insights into the year ahead, and THE ESCAPIST – plus seasonal weekly newspapers and an annual *Drinking & Dining Directory.* Since 2013 we have also been publishing books, like this one, in partnership with Gestalten. Visit *monocle.com/shop.*

5

Radio
Sound approach

Monocle 24 is our round-the-clock radio station that was launched in 2011. It delivers global news and shows covering foreign affairs, urbanism, business, culture, design, print media and more. When you find yourself in Chicago, tune into *Midori House* from midday for a pacy discussion of the day's news. You can listen live or download any of our shows from iTunes, SoundCloud or *monocle.com.*

Priority service
—
Subscribers save 10 per cent in our online shop

Join the club

01
Subscribe to Monocle
A subscription is a simple way to make sure that you never miss an issue – and you'll enjoy many additional benefits.

02
Be in the know
Our subscribers have exclusive access to the entire Monocle archive, and priority access to selected product collaborations, at *monocle.com.*

03
Stay in the loop
Subscription copies are delivered to your door at no extra cost no matter where you are in the world. We also offer an auto-renewal service to ensure that you never miss an issue.

04
And there's more...
Subscribers benefit from a 10 per cent discount at all Monocle shops, including online, and receive exclusive offers and invitations to events around the world.

Choose your package

Premium one year
13 × issues
+ Porter Sub Club bag

One year
12 × issues
+ Monocle Voyage tote bag

Six months
6 × issues

Photographer
Kevin Serna

Still life
David Sykes

Writers
Chloë Ashby
Ari Bendersky
Danielle Braff
Amy Cavanaugh
Melkon Charchoglyan
Robert K Elder
Holly Fisher
Tomos Lewis
Hugo Macdonald
Andrew Mueller
Joe Pickard
Ben Rylan
Brigid Sweeney
Martha Thorne
Jacob Victorine
Toya Wolfe

Images
Alamy
James Caulfield
Freehand Chicago
Tom van Eynde
Adrian Gaut
Grupo Habita
Lula Café
Soho House Chicago
Thomas Hart Shelby

Illustrators
Satoshi Hashimoto
Ceylan Sahin
Tokuma

Monocle
EDITOR IN CHIEF AND
CHAIRMAN
Tyler Brûlé
EDITOR
Andrew Tuck
CREATIVE DIRECTOR
Richard Spencer Powell

CHAPTER EDITING

Need to know
Chloë Ashby

 1
Hotels
Chloë Ashby
Joe Pickard
Holly Fisher

Food and drink
Amy Cavanaugh

Retail
Chloë Ashby

Things we'd buy
Chloë Ashby

Essays
Chloë Ashby

Culture
Holly Fisher

Design and architecture
Joe Pickard

8
Sport and fitness
Danielle Braff

9
Walks
Chloë Ashby

Resources
Chloë Ashby

**The Monocle Travel Guide
Series: Chicago**
GUIDE EDITOR
Chloë Ashby
ASSOCIATE GUIDE EDITORS
Joe Pickard
Holly Fisher
PHOTO EDITOR
Victoria Cagol

**The Monocle Travel Guide
Series**
SERIES EDITOR
Joe Pickard
ASSOCIATE EDITOR
Chloë Ashby
WRITER
Melkon Charchoglyan
DESIGNER
Loi Xuan Ly
PHOTO EDITORS
Matthew Beaman
Victoria Cagol
Shin Miura

Research
Melkon Charchoglyan
Dan Einav
Audrey Fiodorenko
Harriet Kay
Zayana Zulkiflee

Special thanks
Chicago Architecture Center
Choose Chicago
Georgina Godwin
Lauren McGrady
Dan O'Connell
Todd Palmer
Laura Sage

The collection
Planning another trip? We have a global suite of guides, with more set to be released. Cities are fun. Let's explore.

Buy today at all good bookshops

You can also visit the online shops at *monocle.com* and *shop.gestalten.com* to get hold of your copies.

Look out for 'The Monocle Guide to Hotels, Inns and Hideaways'